FLASH!

FLASH!

WRITING THE VERY SHORT STORY

John Dufresne

W. W. NORTON & COMPANY

Independent Publishers Since 1923

NEW YORK | LONDON

For information about permission to reproduce selections from this
book, write to Permissions, W. W. Norton & Company, Inc.,
500 Fifth Avenue, New York, NY 10110

For information about special discounts for bulk purchases, please
contact W. W. Norton Special Sales at specialsales@wwnorton.com
or 800-233-4830

Manufacturing by Berryville Graphics
Book design by Fearn Cutler de Vicq
Production managers: Philip Hofius and Lauren Abbate

ISBN 978-0-393-35235-1 (pbk.)

W. W. Norton & Company, Inc., 500 Fifth Avenue,
New York, N. Y. 10110
www.wwnorton.com
W. W. Norton & Company Ltd., 15 Carlisle Street, London W1D 3Bs

1 2 3 4 5 6 7 8 9 0

For Lefty and Dot
And always for Cindy

*It is my ambition to say in ten sentences
what others say in a whole book.*
—FRIEDRICH NIETZSCHE

Contents

The Intro

LORD CHESTERFIELD called the novel "a kind of abbreviation of a Romance." Ian McEwan described the more compact novella as "the beautiful daughter of a rambling, bloated, ill shaven giant." William Trevor considered the short story "essential art." Writing a story, he said, is infinitely harder than writing a novel, "but it's infinitely more worthwhile." And now we have the even shorter story, a form that was validated, if it needed to be, when Lydia Davis, whose stories are sometimes a sentence long, was awarded the 2013 Man Booker International Prize. In their citation, the judges said of Davis's works: "Just how to categorize them? They have been called stories but could equally be miniatures, anecdotes, essays, jokes, parables, fables, texts, aphorisms or even apothegms, prayers or simply observations."

The short-short story is narrative (or it's not) that is distilled and refined, concentrated, layered, coherent, textured, stimulating, and resonant, and it may prove to be the ideal form of fiction for the twenty-first century, an age of shrinking attention spans and busy and distracted lives, in which our mobile devices connect us to the world as they simultaneously divert us from it. And on the screens of our smartphones and our iPads and our laptops, we can fit an entire work of flash fiction. It's short but not shallow; it's a reduced form used to represent a larger, more complex story; it's pithy and cogent, brief and pointed, and like the gist of a recollected conversation, it offers the essential truth, if not all the inessential facts.

The market for flash fiction is extensive and it's growing. A Google search for flash fiction markets nets 719,000 hits in .55 seconds. *Duotrope* lists 4,700 publications looking for flash fiction, and a few of those outlets publish 365 stories a year. Your chances of finding a home for your short-short story are considerably better than they are for your novel. What better way to break into the world of publishing, to get your name out there, to earn the endorsement of editors, to introduce your beloved characters to an appreciable number of readers? If your dream is to write a novel, consider that flash fiction might be your first small step. I learned to write novels by writing short stories and learned to write short stories by writing very short stories before they had a snappy name.

While flash fiction may be quickly read, it is not often quickly written. Henry David Thoreau wrote, "Not that the story need be long, but it will take a long while to make it short." To be brief takes time. But the obvious fact is that it does take *less* time to write a short-short story than it does the longer forms. It might take years to write a novel (it does for me), months to write a story, but only weeks, maybe days, if you're lucky, to write a very short story. And an occasional morsel of sweet short-term gratification won't make you sick. Promise! With the end so close in sight, you are emboldened, and you learn to finish. If you don't finish, you can't revise, and if you don't revise, you won't learn to write.

Writing flash fiction will teach you to focus. In a short-short story you have no time for digressions, for subplots, for extraneous characters, for backstory. Get in and get out. Start when everything but the action is over, as Frank O'Connor had it. This admirable compression, of course, means that every word carries more weight and every image does double or triple duty. It advances the plot, expresses the theme, and reveals the characters. You learn to take the creative collaboration with your reader to a higher level. You begin the story or the scene, you furnish the clues, sunlight through an open window, say, a woman leaning out, her elbows on the sill, watching the surf pound the beach, and the reader sees the wisp of hair falling over her eye, smells the salt air, hears the sizzle of the surf and the barking of that golden retriever dancing in the waves.

As fiction writers, we are always trying to impose limits on ourselves to avoid the tyranny of the blank page. Flash fiction provides us with a word limit, and that limit may be all we need to get us thinking in an unconventional and creative way. Of limits, the composer Igor Stravinsky said, "The more constraints are imposed, the more one frees oneself of the chains that shackle the spirit . . . and the arbitrariness serves only to obtain precision of execution." And here's what else you get to do with flash fiction: experiment. Follow Lydia Davis's example. Make your flash fictions algebraic word problems or culinary recipes or autocorrected text messages from your estranged father or e-mail spam from Nigerian bankers or advertisements for a new kind of hat that grows hair in just thirty days or for Dr. Campbell's Arsenic Complexion Wafers. In short, anything at all.

I presume you're reading this intro because you want to write stories. (Wanting to write means you're not writing, and that's a prescription for frustration and regret.) Maybe you've already tried. Maybe you've started a novel or two—they're still on your flash drive—but your free time is so limited and your responsibilities so endless. And yet you clearly have not abandoned your literary dream, however modest, however grand. And now you've discovered this relatively new genre that everyone's talking about—the very short story—and you think you might want to give it a try. It's time to scratch that artistic itch. Time to stretch those narrative muscles. Time to test your mettle.

So here's what we'll be doing. We'll demystify the writing process, which may once have seemed intimidating. Writing is work; it's a physical, if sedentary, activity. Writers write even when the writing's not going well—*especially* when the writing's not going well. Writing fiction is not spontaneous or easy. It rewards the patient and the tenacious. It doesn't happen all at once. We'll discuss the craft of storytelling, explore the elements and techniques of short fiction, and examine the qualities that make for vivid and compelling flash fiction. You'll read exemplary short-short stories that will inspire, provoke, and serve as models for your own stories. You'll write up a storm following the prompts and exercises. You'll play with found forms and invent your own. You'll get writing and you'll keep writing. In doing so, you'll make writing a part of your life. You'll learn that your characters, your settings, and your themes are out there in the world. You'll learn to look, to listen, to pay attention, and to notice—the fiction writer's first job. The act of writing itself, you'll realize, the act of making up people you come to care about, the fun of playing with words and with worlds, is its own reward. And the more you write the more you'll want to write.

I hope you're convinced to give it a try. I promise, you're going to have fun. Let us begin.

FLASH!

Briefly

I'm quite interested in the absolute roots of narrative, why we tell stories at all: where the monsters come from.

—Anne Enright

"FOR SALE: baby shoes, never worn." That untitled very short story about the worst thing that can happen in a person's life has been widely and erroneously attributed to Ernest Hemingway and may have its source in a 1910 *Spokane Press* article "Tragedy of Baby's Death Is Revealed in Sale of Clothes." The narrative is over quite suddenly, but the story is not over for the reader.

Writing short-short stories is the art of omission. What you leave out is as important as what you leave in. This is fiction approaching haiku, the art of few words and many suggestions. Like a haiku, these short-short stories start us thinking. The reader then goes on after the piece is finished, goes on in the emotional direction suggested by the story. Think of the very short story as the Zen of fiction—it doesn't explain; it only indicates. It deepens the creative collaboration between author and reader. The story is the call that awaits its response.

The history of fiction has been dominated by the novel and more recently by the novel and the short story. But now there is this seemingly brave new genre around, and, like God, it has many names, and, like Proteus, it takes many forms. I'm talking about very brief fiction, what has been called Sudden, Micro, Skinny, Hyper, Mini, Short-Short, Flash,* Minute, Instant, Nano, Pill-Size, Pocket-Size, Pinhead, Postcard, Hint, Fast, Four-Minute, Smokelong, One-Page, Small, and Furious. These brief fictions have also been called Blasters and Palm-of the-Hand stories. Skippers and Blinks. Drabbles and Dribbles. I suppose the fact that no one can name the beast means that no one knows what it really is. It's short, but even its brevity is in debate. This brevity may be an invitation to undermine the conventions of the traditional short story. It's compact, concentrated, and compressed. It's fifty-five words, or it's fifteen hundred words, or it's somewhere in between. A sentence long? Why not? In the introduction to *Micro Fiction*, editor Jerome Stern posed the question, "Can a short story be too short to be a short story?" By way of an answer, here are two one-sentence stories by Merle Drown:

IN THE CITY

"Fuck you," she explained.

SUFFUSED WITH PLEASURE

She bit him, quick, sharp, precisely, and before he knew it, he said, "I love you."

---

* And since I've chosen to title the book *Flash!*, I want to acknowledge the editorial trio of James Thomas, Denise Thomas, and Tom Hazuka, who coined the term in their 1992 book *Flash Fiction*, published by W. W. Norton.

And now we have Twiction—stories of 140 characters on Twitter. Here's a short-short story by Lynne Barrett that's twenty-two words long and was first posted on Twitter:

DISTANCE

My father, dying, swore his ghost would shake the windows. A thousand miles and thirty years away, tonight he rattles the panes.

And here's a much longer, but still very brief, story from Leonard Nash. It's a comic tale about the things we'll do for love and the things we'll do to get help moving our furniture. It rides along on the dry wit and understatement of our narrator, and there at the heart of the story is the alarming note that seems to illuminate the absurdity that we are privy to.

BEFORE WE DO ANYTHING ELSE

"Fine, I'll sleep with you," Lori said, "but first you have to help me clean out this closet."

Lori had this huge walk-in closet in her hallway. The closet door was opposite the bathroom door. We'd known each other a couple of weeks by this time. We'd met at some raw bar happy hour off the 79th Street Causeway. She had been there with another girl from her office. I'd been there alone.

"Are you moving?" I asked. We were standing in her hallway, surveying the contents of her crowded closet.

"Maybe across town," Lori said.

"How come?" I said.

"I don't want to talk about it," she said.

There were lots of things in Lori's closet. Sanitary products, toilet paper, bed linens, an Electrolux canister vacuum cleaner, her mother's wedding dress, a framed poster of Elvis. Stuff like that she was keeping, but we spent maybe two hours filling liquor boxes and Glad bags with old T-shirts, a pair of matching table lamps that were made to look like pirate ships, stacks of paperback novels, maybe three years' worth of junk mail, old throw pillows, winter clothes from when she lived in Chicago, several dozen shoes, an Anniversary Edition Monopoly game, hundreds of cassette tapes she said she hadn't listened to since high school, and lots more stuff.

"Do you want any of this shit?" Lori said.

"I like the lamps," I said, "but I don't have room for them either."

"I have room for them," she said. "It's just that I don't like them anymore. I never did, actually."

"Why not?" I said.

"Are you going to help me?" she said.

So together we carried the bags and the boxes from the apartment, down the stairs, and put it all by the curb. This was a Sunday afternoon. She said it would all get picked up in the morning.

After we did that, we got into bed and made love for the first time. Had sex. OK, we fucked. Calling it something nice won't change anything. Then we decided to order a pizza, sausage and pepperoni with pineapple chunks. The pineapple was her idea.

"Before we do anything else," Lori said, "we need to inspect the rubber."

"Inspect it for what?" I said.

"For leaks," Lori said. "I've gotten pregnant using these things."

"More than once?"

"Three times."

That seemed like a lot, but who was I to argue with her? So we stood in her bathroom, naked, filling the condom with water from the sink. For a moment I caught the reflection of my own eyes in the mirror and I didn't like what I saw. I turned away and watched as the condom filled slowly. I held it up to the light. The latex sagged with maybe ten ounces of water, about as much water as you'd need for a nice cup of hot tea.

"Add more," she said.

I did like she said, and that condom swelled more than I thought possible, the reservoir tip expanding like a lactating nipple or a child's pacifier. I held it up again. We looked at it.

"That's enough," she said.

"It kind of looks like a bowling pin," I said, "or the breast of a native woman in *National Geographic*—only more translucent."

Lori said it kind of did, and could we order the pizza now.

I suggested we move the condom to the bathtub, fill it up there, see how big it could get.

"This is getting weird," Lori said.

Then she started telling me about her brain tumor. "It's really small," Lori said, "hardly worth mentioning, barely noticeable on the scans, but it's there nonetheless. I could show you the images. The doctor gave me copies."

"Maybe later," I said. I moved the condom over to the tub, supporting the weight of the engorged sack with my left hand, and hooked it onto the spout. I turned on the cold water tap.

"I'm sorry to hear about your tumor," I said. "I hope you'll be all right."

Then Lori told me about this other guy she was seeing now and then. Said he was older than me, that he'd been asking her to marry him, that he'd make for a good husband and father, and that she couldn't decide whether to tell this other guy about her brain tumor.

"It only seems right," I said, "considering the implications of your condition." I wondered if she was suggesting that I would not be a good husband or father. "Have you been intimate with this other guy?"

"I'm hungry," Lori said. "Let's order the pizza already."

"Whatever you want," I said.

She walked out of the bathroom, came back with the cordless phone, and called the pizza place. Now Lori was wearing a pink terry-cloth bathrobe. The number for the pizza place must have been programmed into her speed dial. I saw her press seven and then the pound key. When we were kids, my friends and I called it the tic-tac-toe button. We didn't know what it was for. In our neighborhood, we couldn't even get call waiting in those years, not to mention cable TV. Meanwhile, the condom continued to fill, growing, expanding like a gourd, like a huge papaya right there in the tub. I gripped the rubber-banded opening with two hands as the reservoir tip nudged forward like a wet thumb hitchhiking across the glossy white porcelain of Lori's bathtub.

"How long will it take?" she asked the pizza place. There was a pause. Then she said, "Can you get here any sooner? I'm really hungry." Another pause, and then, "OK, whenever you get here's fine, but the sooner the better."

And then it happened. The condom exploded. Water burst from the shredded latex and careened up the sides of the tub and onto the tile.

"God damn it," Lori screamed as she pulled three yellow hand towels from the stainless steel towel bar mounted on the wall over her wicker clothes hamper. Then she threw them at me. "No, not you," she said into the phone. "Really, I'm fine. It's just this guy."

"Soon as I clean up the floor, I'll put my clothes on and get out of here."

"Please," Lori said, her hand cupped over the receiver. "Please."

Flash fiction is short, but it's not trivial. We're going to explore the world of flash fiction, consider the qualities that make for compelling flash stories, see how they are like traditional short stories and see how they differ. We'll read a wide variety of short-short stories and we'll write our own. We'll write like Chekhov told us to write—serenely, as if we were eating blinis. We've got nothing to prove, but a world to explore. And we'll begin by considering some of our earliest stories—myths.

Telling stories is how we make sense of the world and of our place in it, how we amend our bewilderment. The narrative impulse is embedded in our DNA and seems to be as necessary for our survival as breathing. The seminal storytelling we call myth-making must have begun, I think, with our ancestors' ter-rifying collective aware-ness that this cherished life, this fragile existence, which was all they could know, was going to end for all of them, and was going to end soon. The physical evidence was all around them. Only half the children born reached adulthood; there were few, if any, grandparents. The foods they gathered ripened, spoiled, and then rotted. And at that moment of intolerable real-ization around the campfire, no one uttered a word about the appalling and insidious truth. Maybe they huddled closer, embraced one another, hoping this tenderness would forestall the gathering storm of despair. The obvious and indisputable facts were these: you're born, you struggle, you suffer, you lose the ones you love, you die, you decay, you are soon forgotten. Life is with-out purpose, then. Our being here, our being anywhere, is an accident. Yet here we are. Must we go on? Should we? How do we build a culture in the face of our diminished and dismal future? It's all pointless, isn't it? Senseless.

But we *Homo sapiens* are now and were then creatures who insist on meaning and who abhor enduring chaos. We could not allow this unbearable absurdity of our insignificant existence to stand. At that moment, as our foremothers and forefathers leaned toward the warming fire, out of the grim silence in the dead of night, one voice arose and spoke what others there might have

> Human stories are practically always about one thing, really, aren't they? Death. The inevitability of death.
>
> —*J. R. R. Tolkien*

also been thinking but were too immobilized by doubt and anxiety to utter. "Maybe," the voice said, "maybe we don't die." And we might think of this remarkable leap of the imagination as the moment when civilization began, and we were no longer trapped in time and space.

Another voice said, "If we don't die, where do we go?"

"Home."

And some of those gathered must have looked up at the impossible confusion of stars above them. Home, they thought. What a breathtaking idea. But in order to understand their once and future home, they would need to name it, place it, and populate it. They would need to tell its story, give this amorphous void a shape—a beginning, a middle, and an end. Narrative precedes comprehension. And they knew they could begin anywhere— with a cosmic egg or colored language water or moon blood or a rainbow serpent.

The Sumerians began like this: *Before time began there was only darkness and the goddess Nammu, the primordial sea.* The Greeks: *In the beginning was only chaos. Then out of the void appeared Erebus, the unknowable place where death dwells and Night.* The Zulus: *Long ago before man and animals roamed the earth, there was just darkness and one very large seed.* The Australian Aborigines: *All was darkness in the time before time. The dark land was called Il-ba-lint-ja and it possessed nothing save an endlessly tall pole coming out of the ground.* All of these stories were begun without the knowledge of how they would end, but with a resolute faith in the narrative process. Into all of this darkness, let there be light.

Myth offered a consoling counter-narrative to the bleak realities of daily life, a satisfying and sensible story about our origin and our destiny. Life goes on in some Edenic place other than our own, and to that home we shall return. These creation myths offered both solace and the proof that despite death, disease, dissolution, and destruction, despite random and organized violence, life *does* have meaning, after all, and life *is* worth living.

> All myths are stories, but not all stories are myths: among stories, myths hold a special place.
>
> —Margaret Atwood

And so in this way our ancestors saved themselves from gloom and wretchedness by the power of their imaginations and the evidence of things unseen. Imagination is the faculty that enables us to dream, to remember, to confabulate, to fantasize, that enables us, in other words, to see quite clearly right here in front of our hungry eyes that which is not actually present. Like that sturdy Tree of the Knowledge of Good and Evil in the Garden of Eden with its brown and scaly bark and its allegedly crisp, juicy, and sweet pomaceous fruit, and to see that narrow fellow in the tree, coiled along a slender branch. We wonder what he's up to. We look at him closely, the blunt head, the bifurcated tongue, and the goggle eyes. And then he does something we could not have expected. He whispers into the ear of the woman standing there eyeing the fruit.

Not all myths concerned creation, of course. Some myths tried to explain nature and account for its vicissitudes. There are over five hundred stories of a global flood, for example. The one we may be most familiar with, the one we might think of as a re-creation myth, is the story of Noah, in which God sends the flood because "the wickedness of man was great in the earth." It occurs to us that we may soon be writing yet another inundation story, given global warming and its attendant and accelerating sea-level rise. This time we won't assign divine retribution as the cause, but our own plundering disregard for the planet. The *Guardian* estimates that 700 million people worldwide will be forced to leave their homes by 2050. Thirty-two years from now! The Pacific island nation of Kiribati (formerly the Gilbert Islands) will, in fact, be wiped out before the end of the century. And it won't be the last to go. Its president is now searching for a place to resettle the 103,000 residents. (The Kiribati creation myth begins with a lone spider, asleep and dreaming, and in his dream he hears a voice calling his name, and he wakes and looks down and sees an object: the Earth and the sky sealed together. [And this reminds me of Fredric Brown's very short story within the story "Knock": "The last man on earth sat alone in a room. There was a knock at the door . . ." What's scary here, as Brown points out, is not the knock, but the silence of the ellipsis.])

Other myths explained history, customs, and ethics, established models of desirable behavior. The heroes of these tales were flawed, just as we are, but embodied qualities that we were encouraged to emulate. The heroes were generally kind, generous, hospitable, loyal, prudent, courageous, and selfless. They often had to contend with death-dealing monsters and beasts and with jealous and capricious gods who might suddenly demand a virgin sacrifice or might rape your daughter or command you to murder your own son.

And surely not every story told around the communal fire was a myth. Some stories were told to entertain, like the suspenseful story of the day's treacherous woolly mammoth hunt or the comic tale entitled "Would You Like to Know What Your Kids Did Today While You Were Out Hunting with Your Friends?" But it was the myths that sustained us—have done so for millennia. They are stories we tell over and over, as we are going to do in a moment. But first here's a myth you're no doubt familiar with.

Edith Hamilton tells us that the loquacious mountain nymph Echo fell out of favor with Hera by distracting her with chatter while Hera's philandering husband Zeus stole away. Hera cursed Echo, who could now no longer speak first, but only repeat what was said to her. Echo then fell in love with the beautiful Narcissus, who was only in love with himself, was enraptured by his own reflection in a pool. The scorned Echo faded away until only her voice was left. And Narcissus, who couldn't turn his gaze away from his mirrored image, wasted away.

Maybe you know or can imagine people in your life, here in the twenty-first century, who seem enraptured with themselves or who always have to get in the last word. Maybe you can build a story with mythical resonance for one of them. Daniel Staesser did just that.

NARCISSUS REDEEMED

She worked in one of those boutiques, Twenty-Something Forever or something like that. Backlit, bright pink and silver flourishes festooned the window display with the name of the store scrawled across in a kind of lackadaisical cursive. Racks of jeans, dresses, jackets, all overpriced and undersized. Low pay, long hours, but Didi had worked her way up to management. Maybe it was her sense of style. More likely it was her no-nonsense approach.

Didi could sell condoms in a convent. She had a way of saying exactly what anyone wanted or needed to hear. It was as if she knew their thoughts and could speak them right back in reassurance. But with *him*, the words that usually issued so craftily and with such finality, instead left her breathless.

They had met at that very store. She had caught a peripheral of him staring. It would have been creepy if he hadn't been so cute. He might have been more self-aware, if he hadn't been so aware of himself. He saved face in the moment, not wanting to admit he had been staring at his own reflection. And so their relationship was born on the pretense of attraction, or the reality of it, depending on whom you asked. She *really* was attracted to him. He was *really* attracted to himself.

Cassius welcomed the new relationship like one might embrace a new outfit. Didi looked good on him. He could show her off to family and friends, bring her out sometimes on special occasions, and hang her up when the ennui of the day-to-day threatened the dynamic nature of his personal image. Cassius spent up to four hours a day in the gym, going before and after work. One might think that with all the attention he paid to himself, his career choice would reflect his apparent need to be noticed. Instead of acting or modeling, though, Cassius made a living as a hairstylist, surrounding himself with beauty (and, of course, mirrors) and always striving for a perceived perfection.

As far as Didi was concerned, he had come as close to perfection as one possibly could. She had been as entranced with him from that first auspicious meeting as he had been with himself. The inconvenient truth of his vanity had been lost on Didi, and she found herself only more and more

— Narcissus

Narcissistic attributes

Mirrors everywhere

willing to echo his sentiments, preferences, and habits. Indeed, this fact endeared her to him. And while Cassius didn't embellish Didi with compliments or even sentiment, she nonetheless loved him with a kind of blind fervor.

And so the relationship went for some six months, Didi, Cassius's colorful clown fish, luring coveted attention from other reef-clingers, and Cassius, in turn, an anemone providing protection from a self that Didi had all but forgotten about and that he himself had perhaps never noticed existed.

Then it happened.

It seems sometimes it takes an entire lifetime to forge our identity. It takes hard work, perseverance, and a constant redefinition and reevaluation of self. It takes mistakes, hardships, and sometimes . . . moments. Sometimes these rash and fleeting instances remind us of who we once were and sometimes they help to determine who we become.

The call had come in in the middle of a shift. A Saturday night. The mall was busy—late November, holiday shopping picking up. But as she listened, it all came to an abrupt, unanticipated stop. There was something in his voice.

"I'm sorry," he said. A phrase she had hardly heard him utter in the past, but strangely enough, one that she didn't miss. It had long been a belief of hers that apologizing was too disingenuous. A weakness in character. A denial of humanity. *Forgive and move on.* Maybe this attitude was born from a career spent in retail sales, a bottom-line business. Maybe it was rooted in a fear of failure.

Whatever the case, she hunched over her phone, frozen in the moment.

"Didi, I'm sorry."

"What? What happened? What's wrong?" She could feel the phone shaking in her hand. "Cass? Can you hear me?"

"I made a mistake, Didi."

The possibilities pummeled her, spilling out like sand at first, rough and course, unable to be fully grasped, and then transforming into water, trying to be absorbed, and then gently escaping her fingertips. *Mistake? Sorry for what? Had he been unfaithful? Hurt? Scared? And why hadn't he come to her in person? Had she really expected him to? Still, mistakes were allowed, right? Mistakes could be fixed. Forgive and move on.*

"I . . ." His voice trailed off.

She could sense weakness, an amalgam both emotional and physical. There was a palpable manifestation, a slight vibrato in his voice. Somehow, she felt she knew what he was trying to say, though she tried to deny her intuition by not asking, for fear of the answer she already felt within her. How had she spent so many years knowing exactly what to say, and in the last six months, and even now in this stirring and tautly provocative moment, not be able to formulate the words? She didn't know why, or even how she knew. She didn't even know how *it* happened. She just knew. As suddenly as he had come into her life, he was gone.

Instantly, it struck her that this pariah of perfection had chosen to be selfless in their last moments. And while this might have seemed out of character to anyone else, to Didi it was all she'd ever imagined of him. She spoke into the emptiness on the other end of the line wanting to say, "I love you," but only managing a sobbing echo:

"I . . ."

———

I admire the way Daniel has taken classical figures and set them into that most familiar contemporary American landscape—the mall. And into the workplace, a bottom-line business. And the writing is so smart, so incisive. The malleable Didi looks good on the self-absorbed Cassius; the lackadaisical cursive of the store's sign; overpriced and undersized; the pretense of attraction—so many memorable phrases and pleasurable sentences.

> Do not resist the suddenly irrational in a story; that's imagination at work.
>
> —*F. Scott Fitzgerald*

Made of the Myth

Your turn. Rework a myth of your choosing into a very short story. Go fetch your pen or your pencil and your writing tablet or fire up your computer. And now you get to stare at the blank page or the empty screen for a minute. Paralyzing, isn't it? Perhaps you've been immobilized by this depthless void before. You're thinking, What am I supposed to write about? Well, we know we're going to write about *people* because people are always the subject of fiction (even if they come disguised as halflings or gnomes, goblins or cockroaches), and these made-up people will be troubled because only *trouble* is interesting, and we know we're going to write about *what we don't understand* because that's what fiction writers do.

Let's set seven hundred words as a reasonable goal. In

Edith Hamilton's *Mythology* you'll find stories about the gods and heroes of Greek, Roman, and Norse mythology (Hercules, Prometheus) about love and adventure (Pyramus and Thisbe, Orpheus and Eurydice). You might also check *Bulfinch's Mythology* for your classical stories. Or you can go to the source in Ovid's *Metamorphoses* or *The Iliad* and *The Odyssey* or *The Aeneid*. Or perhaps you prefer Native American myths. If so, refer to *American Hero-Myths, a Study in the Native Religions of the Western Continent* by Daniel G. Brinton. The Bible will serve for Christian myths. At www.americanfolklore.net you can find stories about Pecos Bill, Paul Bunyan, and other heroes. You might want to use the title of the myth as the title of your story. Set the myth-based story in your own contemporary world. Think about people you know or know about. Surely we all know about happily married men in high places who, like Zeus, cannot keep the libido in check, who risk it all (unlike Zeus) for a roll in the hay.

> The problem about art is not finding more freedom, it's about finding obstacles.
>
> —*Richard Rodgers*

Writing exercises like the one above and the others to follow will help you to think in an unhabitual manner. Logic doesn't work in the creative process—not at the start of the process, at any rate. Logic doesn't leap; it plods. Logic is about that which is consistent and non-contradictory. But life is ambiguous, chaotic, inconsistent, and contradictory. You think unhabitually by being arbitrary, not rational. The form of the sonnet is an arbitrary construct. Why fourteen lines? Just because. No reason. No logic. Do it. Writing exercises will teach you to be susceptible to the world and will break the hypnotic and paralyzing spell of the blank page.

Embrace arbitrary constraints. The arbitrary is what will make your story unique. Your arbitrary choices may seem random and irrational, but they will not be erratic and irresponsible.

Stories, Short Stories, and Very Short Stories

All perceiving is also thinking, all reasoning is also intuition, all observation is also invention.

—RUDOLF ARNHEIM

Stories

LET'S TALK about what a short story is before we try to figure out what a very short story is. In fact, let's start with *story*. We run to the *Oxford English Dictionary*. The word comes from the Latin *historia*, history. So this might suggest that a story has happened. It is in the past, as it were. Even if you're writing about the future, in, say, a sci-fi piece, it's a future that's concluded, over, finished. The events *happened* in the future. And maybe this reminds you of Einstein's remark: "The only reason for time to exist is so everything doesn't happen at once." Of course, that notion does away with cause and effect and is, therefore, problematic for the fiction writer. But it also means we're immortal or something like that. And that's good, right? Susan Sontag would append Einstein: "And space exists so that it all doesn't happen to you." Stories, then, might be said, by definition, to have a beginning, middle, and an end, even if time is only a direction in space. Completion. Resolution.

OED definition #1: "A narrative, true or presumed to be true,

[handwritten margin notes: "story", "has", "happened", "Sontag!", "Space exists so that it all doesn't happen to you!"]

relating to important events of celebrated persons of a more or less remote past." This suggestion of truth here (by which, I will presume, they may mean *fact*) suggests that the origin of story-telling may have been an honest recounting of events. "I was in the garden, minding my own business, when Eve handed me a piece of fruit and said she'd just been speaking with this charming and articulate serpent." It's not until definition #5 that the *OED* describes what we writers and readers more commonly think of as a story: "A narrative of real, or more usually, fictitious events, designed for the entertainment of the hearer or reader . . ."

[handwritten margin note: real or imagined]

[handwritten margin note: there must be a point]

Shall we agree that a story is an entertaining and plotted narrative, a related account of an event or events with a beginning, middle, and end? Is any of this up for debate? Need it be entertaining, for instance? Well, why else would you read it? Need it be plotted? Well, yes, unless you have something else that will keep us reading. (In an interview, however, the incomparable William Trevor said, "You don't have to have a plot in a short story, but you do have to have a point. There must be a point to the story." You are making meaning, after all.)

Some stories are long, and when they are, we call them epics or novels or novellas. The *OED* defines a novel as "a fictitious prose narrative of considerable length (now usually one long enough to fill one or more volumes), in which characters and actions representative of the real life of past or present times are portrayed in a plot of more or less complexity." Laurie Henry, in *The Fiction Dictionary*, defines that considerable length as over sixty thousand words, and let me quote: "The novel generally includes a plot, carefully controlled by the writer, comprising a number of episodes. Because of its grander length, a novel will have more characters, take place over a longer period of time, and involve more movement among settings than a novella or short story."

[handwritten: explosion of truth / exclusion of meaninglessness]

Short Stories

Let's consider what some writers of stories have had to say about the form of the short story:

Erskine Caldwell defined it "as an imaginary tale with a meaning, interesting enough to hold the reader's attention, profound enough to express human nature." William Trevor: "If the novel is like an intricate Renaissance painting, the short story is an Impressionist painting. It *should* be an explosion of truth. Its strength lies in what it leaves out just as much as what it puts in. It is concerned with the total exclusion of meaninglessness."

As to this matter of leaving out, Ernest Hemingway had this to say in *Death in the Afternoon*: "If a writer of prose knows enough about what he is writing about he may omit things that he knows and the reader, if the writer is writing truly enough, will have a feeling of those things as strongly as though the writer had stated them. The dignity of movement of an ice-berg is due to only one-eighth of it being above water. A writer who omits things because he does not know them only makes hollow places in his writing." *[handwritten margin: writer may omit what he knows bc the reader will fill it in]*

And in a letter to his friend and editor Aleksey Suvorin, Anton Chekhov explained: "Of course it would be pleasant to combine art with a sermon, but for me personally it is extremely difficult and almost impossible, owing to the conditions of technique. You see, to depict horse-thieves in seven hundred lines I must all the time speak and think in their tone and feel in their spirit; otherwise, if I introduce subjectivity, the image becomes blurred and the story will not be as compact as all short stories ought to be. When I write, I reckon entirely upon the reader to add for himself the subjective elements that are lacking in the story."

A short story is made up. It's fiction even if it's based on actual incidents. It tends to be realistic—about this John Gardner has much to say in *The Art of Fiction*. It's concerned with character. It has, as we've said, a beginning, a middle, and an end. Maybe it has a plot. It needs to be entertaining. And maybe plot is a key to entertainment. E. M. Forster, in *Aspects of the Novel*, wrote, "Yes–oh dear yes–the novel tells a story." And went on wonderfully to explain the need for plot: "Neanderthal man listened to stories . . . The primitive audience was an audience of shock-heads, gaping around the campfire, fatigued with contending against the mammoth or the wooly rhinoceros, and only kept awake by suspense. What would happen next? The novelist droned on, and as soon as the audience guessed what happened next, they either fell asleep or killed him. We can estimate the dangers incurred when we think of the career of Scheherazade in somewhat later time. Scheherazade avoided her fate because she knew how to wield the weapon of suspense—the only literary tool that has any effect upon tyrants and savages."

Perhaps Forster's key word here is *suspense*, the pleasurable excitement and anticipation regarding an outcome. That's what plot affords the reader. We don't know where we're going, and we're desperate to find out. And that's a good thing. Plot suggests that this tale we're reading is a journey we're on, that each narrative step we take leads to the next step, and that all of our trudging will carry us to the story's ultimate destination, which, for now, remains a mystery. A plot makes the reader want to know what happens next.

Forster also said this about plot: "A plot is also a narrative of events, the emphasis falling on causality—'The king died and then the queen died' is a story. But 'the king died and then the queen died of grief' is a plot. The time-sequence is preserved, but the sense of causality overshadows it."

So perhaps we can agree, then, that a short story is a fictional prose narrative meant to entertain, and it's about people. It has, as I've mentioned more than once, a beginning, a middle, and an end. It's shorter than a novel, shorter than a novella; it's economic, inferential, allusive because it must do so much in so brief a time and space; it changes our lives somehow.

Virginia Woolf wrote in *To the Lighthouse*: "What is the meaning of life? . . . The great revelation had never come. The great revelation perhaps never did come. Instead there were little daily miracles, illuminations, matches struck unexpectedly in the dark." Maybe that will serve for now as a definition of the short story: little miraculous illuminations, matches struck unexpectedly in the dark. And we should heed Flannery O'Connor's words: "Being short does not mean being slight. A short story should be long in depth and should give us an experience of meaning . . ." A story is good when you continue to see more and more in it, and when it continues to escape you.

> A plot first meant a physical site and building plan, then the stage director's plot or blocking plan, then the action or story blocked out.
>
> —*Edward O. Wilson*

Very Short Stories

The very short story isn't new. We've had Kafka's *Parables and Paradoxes* and Borges's *Ficciones*, among others. And at the turn of the last century *McClure's* magazine, which billed itself as a magazine for women, began to publish "Daily Shorts," very short stories. In 1926, *Collier's Weekly* began printing a one-page narrative that it subtitled "short-short story." The magazine gave impetus to the revival of the form. *Cosmopolitan* followed *Collier's*. It published the likes of Somerset Maugham and A. J. Cronin. But then the form fell out of favor until the boost it seems to have gotten more recently from the Internet and its need for and/or fondness for concise narrative.

We've had anecdotes and jokes and biblical parables, of course, like this:

THE PRODIGAL SON

And he said, A certain man had two sons: And the younger of them said to his father, Father, give me the portion of goods that falleth to me. And he divided unto them his living. And not many days after the younger son gathered all together, and took his journey into a far country, and there wasted his substance with riotous living. And when he had spent all, there arose a mighty famine in that land; and he began to be in want. And he went and joined himself to a citizen of that country; and he sent him into his fields to feed swine. And he would fain have filled his belly with the husks that the swine did eat: and no man gave unto him. And when he came to himself, he said, How many hired servants of my father's have bread enough and to spare, and I perish with hunger! I will arise and go to my father, and will say unto him, Father, I have sinned against heaven, and before thee, And am no more worthy to be called thy son: make me as one of thy hired servants. And he arose, and came to his father. But when he was yet a great way off, his father saw him, and had compassion, and ran, and fell on his neck, and kissed him. And the son said unto him, Father, I have sinned against heaven, and in thy sight, and am no more worthy to be called thy son. But the father said to his servants, Bring forth the best robe, and put it on him; and put a ring on his hand, and shoes on his feet: And bring hither the fatted calf, and kill it; and let us eat, and be merry: For this my son was dead, and is alive again; he was lost, and is found. And they began to be merry. Now his elder son was in the field: and as he came and drew nigh to the house, he heard musick and dancing. And he called one of the servants, and asked what these things meant. And he said unto him, Thy brother is come; and thy father hath killed the fatted calf, because he hath received him safe and sound. And he was angry, and would not go in: therefore came his father out, and intreated him. And he answering said to his father, Lo, these many years do I serve thee, neither transgressed I at any time thy commandment: and yet thou never gavest me a kid, that I might make merry with my friends. But as soon as this thy son was come, which hath devoured thy living with harlots, thou hast killed for him the fatted calf. And he said unto him, Son, thou art ever with me, and all that I have is thine. It was meet that we should make merry, and be glad: for this thy brother was dead, and is alive again; and was lost, and is found.

And from *Aesop's Fables*:

THE LION IN LOVE

A Lion once fell in love with a beautiful maiden and proposed marriage to her parents. The old people did not know what to say. They did not like to give their daughter to the Lion, yet they did not wish to enrage the King of Beasts. At last the father said: "We feel highly honored by Your Majesty's proposal, but you see our daughter is a tender young thing, and we fear that in the vehemence of your affection you might possibly do her some injury. Might I venture to suggest that Your Majesty should have your claws removed, and your teeth extracted, then we would gladly consider your proposal again." The Lion was so much in love that he had his claws trimmed and his big teeth taken out. But when he came again to the parents of the young girl they simply laughed in his face, and bade him do his worst.

We've had Zen koans, this one by Ekai:

NOT THE WIND, NOT THE FLAG

Two monks were arguing about a flag. One said: "The flag is moving."

The other said: "The wind is moving."

The sixth patriarch happened to be passing by. He told them: "Not the wind, not the flag; mind is moving."

So just what is a short-short story? In *The Fiction Dictionary*, Laurie Henry takes a stand: a complete story of 1,500 words max and around 250 words minimum. "For a short-short story to seem complete in itself and not just an outline for a longer piece,

[handwritten: Short stories but around an idea or theme]

some aspect must be omitted—and often what is omitted is a complex plot. [This brings to mind Borges, who wrote: 'Writing a plot summary makes the writing of the actual book a needless extravagance.'] Many short-short stories, in fact, are built around a theme or an idea rather than a plot; others basically are composed of exposition."

And now that Borges has insinuated himself into our discussion with what can only be described as a call for very short novels, let's try one. I'll start. Several years ago, a few of us were sitting around on a Friday night at a metal picnic table in the breezeway of the second floor of AC 2 at Florida International University, talking about stories, when one of us told a long and tangled tale about a woman he knew in Ireland who was twice spurned by the same man with whom she was desperately in love. I asked the storyteller if he was going to write that story, and he said no. I thought about the story for years, but never wrote it until I was asked to write a very short story for a local art project called "Downtown Miami: The Land Beneath Our Feet." I saw this as my chance to write the novel that I'd been so long ruminating over. Not Ireland, but South Florida. Here it is.

FRAGILE: A NOVEL

I

Before Kate's parents died (Spanish influenza), they had feared that Kate, a homely girl by her own plucky estimation, would not find a husband, so they sent her off to secretarial college in Tampa. That was 1918. Now it's 1925 and she's dating Mr. Alan Hays, the assistant postmaster at the downtown Miami post office. Kate is head over heels, and so is Mr. Hays, if his lavish attentions are an honest indication. He has conducted a solicitous and chaste courtship, rather more chaste than necessary, Kate thinks, But he isn't ready to settle down, not just yet. He's married, he likes to say, to his job. He also dates Frieda Luft, but only on occasion, and only casually.

II

On their strolls through the new Bayfront Park, Kate and Mr. Hays discuss European history and metaphysics. Evenings, they sit in the library at her residential hotel on Flagler, and he reads Herodotus to her. She reads Emily Dickinson to him. One day, he tells her, he'll enter politics, maybe run for governor. He says it out loud: Governor Alan Hays. Kate smiles and tries to imagine herself in Tallahassee. Another day, he takes Kate on an architectural tour of the neoclassical post office building. He points out all the gratuitous stylistic details: the monumental pilasters, the arched openings, the cartouches, the enriched entablature. That's culture, he tells Kate, doing what we don't have to do. When Frieda gets pregnant, Mr. Hays does what he has to do and marries her. They buy a house in Coconut Grove. Kate is heartbroken.

III

And still in love. Mr. Hays hires Kate as his secretary. She is, after all, the smartest woman he knows. She grows accustomed to this new intimacy. She is very much his wife at work. The clerks, a man from up north and a young woman who is a great favorite with the customers, defer to Kate. Mr. Hays and Frieda raise three boys, and when the oldest is ten, Frieda dies in childbirth. Kate arrives to comfort Mr.

Hays. She arranges care for the baby, manages the funeral, ensconces herself in the home as the choreographer of grief and condolences. Over the ensuing weeks, she cooks meals, sees to the children's well-being, supervises the nanny. She stays late to read to the bereaved widower, and soon they have fallen into their old conversations about the Great War and the meaning of life.

IV

Kate knows that soon enough Mr. Hays, now the esteemed postmaster, will see that he needs a wife, a helpmeet and boon companion. She plans for the inevitable and desirable upheaval in her life. Mr. Hays returns to work and asks the young clerk, Sara, now in her thirties, to marry him. Kate now understands the difference between despair and fear, between the wreck and what follows in its wake. She imagines a future—empty and endless. She vacates her position at the post office.

V

After two years of marriage, Sara drinks a bottle of Kwik-Deth insect poison. Kate attends the wake. In the visitation room, she offers her sympathies to the bereaved widower and tells him that when she gave up hope, only then did she begin to live again. Mr. Hays tells her that she was the one he cared about all along; surely she knew that; she is his equal—the obscene implication being that he would not marry a woman he could not overshadow. He tells Kate that Frieda and Sara took care of his physical requirements, and she, Kate, took care of his intellectual needs. When he proposes a resumption of their invigorating friendship, she slaps his face and tells him it's too bad he felt the need to separate his desires and tells him as well that he has no right to insult those pitiable women. She says, Decency is the soul of culture, Mr. Hays.

Long Story. Short

Now it's your turn. You've got notes for a novel somewhere in that desk drawer or in a computer file. It's a weight you feel when you're away from the writing desk. It seems so daunting, doesn't it? You'll need months to come up with a decent draft, if you're lucky, and years to finish the tale. Not anymore. Take out those notes and write your summarized novel in, let's say, a thousand words. You'll finish it, a draft of it, this week. The exercise might even encourage you to begin the long march that is the writing of the conventional novel.

Is it flash fiction, you might ask, or is it prose poetry? *The Princeton Handbook of Poetic Terms* defines a prose poem as "a composition able to have any and all features of the lyric, except that it's put on the page . . . as prose. [It differs from] short prose in that it has, usually, more pronounced rhythm, sonorous effects, imagery, and density of expression." Of course, as a fiction writer, I like to think that fiction has to do everything that a poem does—the precision, the music, the vivid imagery, etc.—do all of that plus tell a story. Narrative drive, then, would seem to be something you ask of a short-

short that you might not expect or need from a prose poem. I asked three friends, poets all, for their thoughts on the matter, and they each replied with what I'll call short-short stories. Here's what Denise Duhamel wrote:

POETRY OR PROSE?

Prose poetry and flash fiction are kissing cousins. They are kissing on *Jerry Springer*, knowing they're cousins, and screaming, "So what?" as the audience hisses. They're kissing on *One Life to Live*, unaware one's aunt is the other's mother. A prose poem suffers from amnesia, and when her friends tell her about her past, nothing they describe produces in her even a flicker. In a flash, she thinks: They are wrong—something tells me I was once a short short. Flash fiction looks into the mirror and sees a prose poem. A prose poem parts his hair on the left instead of the middle, and his barber tells him he's flash fiction. A prose poem walks into a bar, and the bartender says, "What'll you have? The usual paragraph?" A flash fiction walks into the doctor's office and the doctor says, "How's that stanza feeling?" There may be a difference between flash fiction and prose poems, but I believe the researchers still haven't found the genes that differentiate them.

––––––––––

And Julie Marie Wade distinguishes a prose poem from a work of short creative nonfiction from a work of very short fiction:

Y (PROSE POEM)

Little letter I could not love. Vowel & consonant, chromosome & question. How frugal & elusive you have been! Always the middleman: *xyz, xyz*, never the workers or the bourgeoisie. Also the musicman: *xylophone & lyre*. At times I find your histrionics almost unbearable—a new age of *womyn & wyne*. Too haughty for the twenty-fifth place, you stand like V on a stilt, on a pedestal stair, touting your yowling message. Inverted tripod. Impotent slingshot. (David's one-time triumphant tool.) And what a spy you are, your cunning infiltrations: *dys-trophy, dys-functional, dys-phoria*. How could I ever catch you? Stealthy somnambulist, chameleon of stick limbs & curlicues. You reduce nouns to improper adjectives with these easy recipes: *smirk-y, pith-y, weight-y, greed-y. Lad* into *lady*. That's your fix, your sing-song-y resonance. Usurper of the second person. Pseudonym for stranger. You & yours assaulting me & mine through triangle lips split open, isosceles. Take your tuning-fork face & turn it into the light. Make your inquiry, outspoken & asinine. *Yawn, yang, yammer*. An active force in the universe. Tell me I'm boring you. Call me *yellow*. Tempt me with *yams*, sweetened to marshmallow pudding. Or come in second: *axis, coordinate, unknown quantity*. Occasionally, impressed with your arrogance, I've let you *yo-yo* me—lift up my skirts, my songs, *buoy* me again in the wrong direction. Invention: the crafty voice in the back of the head, making suggestions. Or the picture on the grade school wall, building associations. *Y is for yak*, a long-haired, humped Tibetan ox, & *you* who are never what you are.

Y (MICRO-MEMOIR/MICRO-ESSAY/FLASH NONFICTION)

Like most children, I asked "why?" incessantly. Why could we have breakfast for dinner—those sometimes-nights with waffles hot from the griddle, bacon oozing grease on a paper towel, orange juice thawing from concentrate in the pitcher—but no pork chops with applesauce at 8 a.m., no burgers or pizza or popcorn with *The Price is Right*? My questions only got harder as I grew: Why was God real and Santa Claus make-believe? Why did some kids get cancer and have to live at St. Jude's? Why could my mother have only one child when she always said she wanted two or three? Surely my parents yearned to distract me, or to tell me to shut my trap—*why couldn't I learn keep my questions, like my hands, to myself?* Instead, my father was fond of quipping, "If *y* is the question, then *z* must be the answer." We even tried it that way. A figure I couldn't calculate became *zero*. An animal I didn't recognize turned out to be a *zebra*, of course. If it was hard to spell and easy to mispronounce, then it must have been a *zyzzyva* or a *zephyr*. And any recitation gone wrong: *zip-a-dee-doo-dah*. In college, I wanted to major in Inquiry, but the counselor wouldn't let me. I had to sign up for *Zoology* and *Zen Buddhism* instead.

Y (MICRO-FICTION/SHORT-SHORT/FLASH FICTION)

Yves was a quiet boy often mistaken for a girl: *Yves* was assumed to be *Eve* and sometimes listed as such on the roster. What made it worse was that Yves was from Eden, Idaho, and attended school in the much larger Twin Falls. His teachers had a habit of asking, "Is Eve here—Eve from Eden?" This always made the other kids laugh, and Yves crimsoned with embarrassment, shrinking deeper and deeper in his chair. At the start of sixth grade, which was the start of middle school, which might as well have been the start of everything that mattered in life, Yves summoned his courage and announced in Homeroom, "Please call me Y from now on." "Y?" Mr. Benson repeated, giving his suspenders a tug. "Because I asked nicely," Yves replied, and everyone laughed. This time it was a laugh of affirmation, and Yves found himself perking up a little. "Well, I can't just call you after a letter," Mr. Benson sighed. Now Yves sat straight as a pencil, his hair red as the eraser on top. No one could miss the gleam in his eyes as he countered, "But, Mr. Benson, why not?"

———

And Campbell McGrath:

THE PROSE POEM

On the map it is precise and rectilinear as a chessboard, though driving past you would hardly notice it, this boundary line or ragged margin, a shallow swale that cups a simple trickle of water, less rill than rivulet, more gully than dell, a tangled ditch grown up throughout with a fearsome assortment of wildflowers and bracken. There is no fence, though here and there a weathered post asserts a former claim, strands of fallen wire taken by the dust. To the left a cornfield carries into the distance, dips and rises to the blue sky, a rolling plain of green and healthy plants aligned in close order, row upon row upon row. To the right, a field of wheat, a field of hay, young grasses breaking the soil, filling their allotted land with the rich, slow-waving spectacle of their grain. As for the farmers, they are, for the most part, indistinguishable: here the tractor is red, there yellow; here a pair of dirty hands, there a pair of dirty hands. They are cultivators of the soil. They grow crops by pattern, by acre, by foresight, by habit. What corn is to one, wheat is to the other, and though to some eyes the similarities outweigh the differences it would be as unthinkable for the second to commence planting corn as for the first to switch over to wheat. What happens in the gully between them is no concern of theirs, they say, so long as the plow stays out, the weeds stay in the ditch where they belong, though any-one would notice the wind-sown cornstalks poking up their shaggy ears like young lovers run off into the bushes, and the kinship of these wild grasses with those the farmer cultivates is too obvious to mention, sage and dun-colored stalks hanging their noble heads, hoarding exotic burrs and seeds, and yet it is neither corn nor wheat that truly flourishes there, nor some jackalopian hybrid of the two. What grows in that place is possessed of a beauty all its own, ramshackle and unexpected, even in winter, when the wind hangs icicles from the skeletons of briars and small tracks cross the snow in search of forgotten grain; in the spring the little trickle of water swells to welcome frogs and minnows, a muskrat, a family of turtles, nesting doves in the verdant grass; in summer it is a thoroughfare for rac-coons and opossums, field mice, swallows and blackbirds, migrating egrets, a passing fox; in autumn the geese avoid its abundance, seeking out windrows of toppled stalks, fat-ter grain more quickly discerned, more easily digested. Of those that travel the local road, few pay that fertile hollow any mind, even those with an eye for what blossoms, vetch and timothy, early forsythia, the fatted calf in the fallow field, the rabbit running for cover, the hawk's descent from the lightning-struck tree. You've passed this way yourself many times, and can tell me, if you would, do the formal fields end where the valley begins, or does everything that surrounds us emerge from its embrace?

We'll give Charles Simic the last word on this subject. "The prose poem is the result of two contradictory impulses, prose and poetry, and therefore cannot exist, but it does. This is the sole instance we have of squaring the circle."

And here are a couple of short-short stories that square the circle by utilizing traditional poetic forms. The first, by Brenda Miller, uses the pantoum, a fifteenth century Malaysian folk poem form.

PANTOUM FOR 1979

I'm twenty years old, barely an adult, my belly flat—though inside that belly a baby is growing. Or not a baby: a *something*, a cluster of cells lodged in the fallopian tubes. In a few weeks I'll be in pain, like a penknife stabbing again and again. But for now I'm just a girl in a broken-down Toyota, moving her few belongings into a room in a big red house on the hill.

Not a baby, I'll remind myself later, just a cluster of cells, lodged where it didn't belong. I must have found this house from a tacked message on a bulletin board on campus, an index card with a man's spidery handwriting looking for boarders. For now I'm just a girl, broken down, with few belongings to move into this big red house on the hill. I got the room set apart from all the others, with no windows, in the back.

I must have found this house from a tacked message on a bulletin board, after seeing the run-down hippie pads in Arcata, the cluttered trailer in McKinleyville. This house, in Blue Lake, four miles inland, lies just beyond the fog line that descends on coastal towns. I chose the room set apart: no windows, in the back. The bus runs several times a day and stops just at the foot of this hill.

This house, in Blue Lake, lies just beyond the fog line that descends on coastal towns. I'm carrying in some battered boxes of books, a suitcase of clothes, photo albums, a hippie bedspread, some thin pillows. The bus stops with a hiss at the foot of the hill. My new roommate, Francisco—short, dark, a blue headband tied around his forehead—comes up the drive and asks if I need help.

He carries in a box of battered books, a suitcase, photo albums, my hippie bedspread, and some thin pillows. He smiles a half-smile that reveals bright, small teeth. He wears a blue headband, and his name is *Francisco*, not Frank. He smells of tobacco and something else I can't quite pinpoint: sage perhaps, the smell of the desert.

That half-smile reveals bright, small teeth. We're in red-wood country, and the damp bark of the big trees rises all around us, canopies high overhead filled with birds: red-tailed hawks, ospreys, flickers, and ravens. Yet, he smells of tobacco and the desert. The ravens call raucously, as if in warning, *caw! caw! caw!*

We're in redwood country, and the birds flock like omens: hawks, ospreys, flickers, and ravens. I'll lie in my bed in that dark-paneled room, aware of Francisco and his energy pulsing in a room on the other side of the house. The ravens wake me up with their *caw! caw! caw!* We'll play basketball together, and he'll dribble the ball by me, touch me just once on the hip with the back of his hand.

Later I'll lie in my bed in that dark-paneled room, aware—so aware—of Francisco on the other side of the house. In my mouth, the taste of honey; in my knees, an ache. He touched me just once on the hip with the back of his hand. That's all it took to determine what happened next.

In my mouth the taste of honey. I baked loaves and loaves of bread for all the boys in that house after the baby—the cluster of cells—was gone. That's all it takes sometimes: the crust of chewy bread and pats of butter to melt on the tongue. In the redwoods, he gave me the name Little Raven. I baked loaves and loaves of bread for the boys in that house after the baby was gone. I was twenty years old, barely an adult. On my tongue, the name Little Raven, a bird that seemed like a sentinel. The pain, like a penknife, stabbing again and again.

The author casts a spell with hypnotic repetition and lyrical prose. This is a deceptively complex story of a pair of lodgers ("lodged where it didn't belong"), of gain and loss, relief and regret, and ironically a story of rebirth. Here are birds that warn, birds that foresee, birds that protect, birds that connect the natural world and a more mysterious world.

Tom DeMarchi's short-short story is an abecedarian, an ancient poetic, and here prose, form. Generally, the first line (or sentence, in this case) begins with the first letter of the alphabet and successive ones begin with correspondingly successive letters, until the final letter is reached.

MILK OF MAGNESIA

As soon as Steve limps out of CVS, the nagging regret he'd felt just moments earlier while shoving a bottle of Milk of Magnesia down his pants for Paul, Anna's constipated father, disappears, and not only because he thinks he eluded the security guard's steely gaze, but also because he sees Anna sitting in her Mercury, parked right where they'd planned—next to the Wachovia ATM on the far side of T.J. Maxx—and her pink-streaked blond hair gives Steve's heart a little jolt of electricity. Before getting laid off from his job in the Coca-Cola warehouse thirteen months ago, Steve'd never stolen anything in his life, but what with the unemployment checks running out and Steve swallowing his pride and agreeing to move in with Paul, and then Paul getting bound up from a gastroenterological collision of diverticulitis and too much of the food bank's government-issue cheese, and Anna being six months pregnant (a boy, yet unnamed) and having her hours cut at Shear Joy Hair Salon, well, he'd had to make some compromises in the ethics department, and that was both okay and not okay with Steve, depending on his mood, and depending on how full his stomach was and how much he thought about the cells dividing in Anna's womb and how those cells were forming a son whose overall health and well-being would, sooner than later, depend on Steve's ability to provide a suitable and abundant environment conducive to raising a family.

CVS's doors whoosh open behind him, and before Steve makes it to Anna's car he hears a deep voice say, "You wanna show me what you got in those pants, sir? Don't even think of running, 'cause I was the state champ in the hundred-yard dash back in high school, and you best believe my feet've still got wings."

Even if he hadn't slipped and twisted his ankle in the bathtub last week and he'd sprinted safely to the car, Steve knows a license plate can't outrun anyone's pen.

For a moment Steve weighs his two options—run or stay—neither of which can lead to anything good, so he turns and notices two things about the security guard: his name tag says "Xavier," and Xavier's wearing a wedding ring, and this reminds Steve of his own ring that he hocked two months ago to buy the Mercury a new timing belt.

"Guard" is an odd title for Xavier's job, since he doesn't guard things; on a good day he might intimidate kids from pocketing gum. He stands in plain sight to remind would-be criminals that there's an order to things, and so his presence is at best an appeal to our better angels and at base a threat of consequences, yet Xavier's hangdog expression betrays the weight of his own compromises. Instead of running, Steve wonders about Xavier's abandoned ambitions—did he one day dream of being a lawyer or a cop?—and he remembers that in fifth grade—for that hunchbacked nun, Sister Lorraine—he'd written an essay about wanting to be a cop himself.

Just then Steve notices Xavier's hand resting on the mace.

"Keep calm, Xavier," he says.

"Look here, sir," Xavier says, "I know you got more than a dick in your pants. Me and you, we gotta go inside and straighten things out."

Never before had Steve's mouth been so dry; it feels as if his tongue has fallen asleep on the beach. Over his shoulder, he hears the Mercury's rattling tailpipe. "Please," he says, "this isn't who I am."

Quite against his better judgment, Steve backs toward the edge of the curb, where he senses the car has pulled up and parked, and without taking his eyes off Xavier, he reaches back and feels the passenger door handle; he raises it and pulls the door open, slides inside, and closes it—all the while keeping his eyes locked with Xavier's. Right then, as the Mercury inches away from the curb, Xavier steps forward, his hands extended flat, a gesture Steve decides is a wave goodbye rather than a command to halt. Something about the flattened palms and the lumbering gait tells Steve that Xavier is granting him a reprieve, and so Steve feels obligated to point to Anna's protruding belly as if to say, "Who I am is bigger than this moment."

The image of Xavier recedes in the side-view mirror, and Steve chokes back the bile rising in his throat.

Until this moment, Steve has kept the Milk of Magnesia jocked; he looks at Anna, who smiles sadly while he unzips his fly, uncaps the bottle, takes a swig, and thinks about the near and distant future:

Very soon, they'll be back in the apartment, and Paul will gulp down the Milk of Magnesia without saying thanks or asking where they'd gotten the money to buy it, and Steve will wonder whether Xavier will have to explain himself to his boss, whether he'll lose his job, and whether he'll go home and tell his wife about the most pathetic shoplifter ever to enter the store.

Will Xavier remember this day with regret or pride? Xavier might forget the incident altogether, but Steve knows he'll remember for the rest of his life.

Years from now, when he's a father and today is nothing more than one peak in a range of shames, Steve hopes he'll have forgiven himself and will have the capacity to extend to his son the mercy all children require.

Zipping up his fly, Steve decides that one day he'll make Xavier proud.

———————

You can see how much fun Tom was having with the wild and robust sentences to begin the story. Will we ever get through the alphabet at this rate? And look at all the stories in play: Steve, a desperate man taking desperate measures, out of work and out of luck; Anna, pregnant and living hand-to-mouth; Paul, constipated and somewhat helpless. And Xavier, security guard at a convenience store, a man who might have been a contender.

In his introduction to *Short Shorts: An Anthology of the Shortest Stories*, first published in 1982, Irving Howe sketches out a few variations of the short shorts. The first variation he calls *One Thrust of Incident*. In these very short stories, the time span, he writes, is "extremely brief, a few hours, maybe even a few minutes: Life is grasped in symbolic compression." Epiphanies out of context, he says of this variation. The reader supplies the context, which, if it were present, would make the short story a long story.

Corey Ginsberg gives us a glimpse of a marriage in crisis. Or has the crisis long passed? A marriage of lassitude and festering bitterness.

PLAYING THE PART

"You always have to play the part, don't you?" she slurs at his image in the bathroom mirror with her third-glass-of-wine inflection.

"Maybe I do." He adjusts the cuff links on his sky-blue shirt, the cuff links she likes to remind him cost nearly half as much as her wedding ring. "Maybe we both do."

They're late as usual—about to cross the line from fashionably tardy to awkward-entrance-unavoidable-stares-fake-apology late. Not that she cares; it's just another one of his work things, another wine-and-cheese-wasn't-it-a-beautiful-day-today-not-a-cloud-in-the-sky cocktail hour that will end with the inevitable promise of dinner parties and weekend trips to the mountains for skiing that won't ever happen. It will end like they all end—with a car ride of switched radio stations, speeding through yellow lights, and the endless stream of half-smoked cigarettes flung into the puckering black night. It will end with his side of the bed and her side of the bed, with a perfectly timed tugging match for the comforter, with a parade of hours on the red face of the alarm clock stepping rhythmically toward dawn.

He's pacing, glancing at his watch as she puts on mascara. But her earrings clash with the paisley pattern on her skirt. She takes a hearty swig of wine and searches through her jewelry box for a better match. Maybe the silver hoops. Or diamond studs.

"I'm going downstairs to warm up the car."

"Be right there." As his dress shoes clomp down the stairs, she lights a cigarette and studies her reflection. It's the skirt that's wrong, not the earrings. After a long drag, she rests the cigarette on the edge of the dresser and heads into the closet. So many patterned prints hanging along the back wall—nearly a dozen that match her shoes.

She lies on the shag carpet beneath the weight of too many decisions, staring up at a row of blouses and sweaters that hang in a perfect line along the back wall. The car engine rumbles its reprise from the silence while her skirt collects wrinkles. She stares up at the shirtsleeves—slender fabric tubes—and imagines they're telescopes showing her the view of a world millions of light-years away.

———

What misery! What a hopeless wreck of a marriage! Even the agitated hyphens contribute to the dire depiction of these lives lived in harrowing misery. Our wife will find no solace or salvation in her closeted stuff; she'll find no victory in the battle of radio stations, and no escape in the glasses of wine. And the cigarette— it's still burning at the edge of the dresser. Here Corey is trying to tell a larger story in a smaller space by using exposition, primarily. She's expecting you to imagine the missing, the elliptical, plot. She presents a moment in a marriage and you construct its history. She tells the story of an ill-fated evening out, and you imagine the longer story that you call "Marriage" or "Telescopes." The struggle is mostly off the page, is not so much happening as it has happened and will continue to happen.

> The shorter the piece of fiction, the less need for a plot. You can write a fine story in which little happens: A man curses his neighbor, a widow quits her mahjongg group, or an unhappy family goes on a picnic. Simple shapes work better than something fussy and complicated.
>
> —*Jerome Stern*

Now it's your turn to write a One Thrust of Incident story. Let's consider the brief time span. The story might happen on a walk down the naughty aisle at the supermarket or on a ride up an escalator at the mall or during a yoga class on the beach or at a business lunch at Joe's Stone Crab or on a flight from New York to Boston, but with Corey's story in mind, let's write about a bride's walk down the aisle at her wedding on the happiest day of her life, and we'll call it . . .

The Marriage Knot

Why not set the wedding in a church, maybe one that you're familiar with, so you can take advantage of the religious iconography and add a touch of solemnity to the joyous occasion? Before you write a word, take a closer look around the church. Note the source of the light. (Pouring through the clerestory windows?) Look up at the ceiling. (A fresco of the Resurrection?) At the floor of the nave. What do you hear? (Throat-clearing in the choir loft?) What do you smell? (The cones of roses clipped to the pew ends?) Cue the music. (Mendelssohn's "Wedding March"?) Your story begins when the bride takes her first step toward the altar. Put yourself in her head. See what she sees; feel what she feels; think what she thinks. You're looking for the trouble that is at the heart of this and every story, the trouble here suggested by the noun "knot" in the title: an intertwining, a complication, and specifically, in matrimonial terms, "the *bond* of wedlock." Something tells her that this is not what she wants for her life at all. What was the image that triggered this unsettling revelation? The smile on the groom's face? The scent of her father's cologne? The story ends when her procession down the aisle ends. But how it ends is up to you. The walk she takes today is the walk she will take for the rest of her days. That's what she thinks.

Howe's second variation he calls *Life Rolled Up*. In these brief stories "you get the illusion of sustained narrative, since they deal with lives over an extended period of time; but, actually, these lives are so compressed into *typicality and paradigm*, the result seems very much like a single incident." *Life as a treadmill*, always walking, never going anywhere. Tom Williams has written a story that fits this definition.

EMERGENCY CASH

My gold card fails to impress.

The four hundred dollars in my father's wallet, however, lure Aaron's eyes from his cell phone. "You keep that all the time?" he says.

"Emergencies," my father says, brown eyes sage, silver in his beard and close-cropped hair. He extends one frail bill. Ben Franklin needs to rediscover electricity to stay awake. "Your great-grandfather's," my father says.

"Cool." Aaron pockets his phone, reaches for the bill. The touch of money is foreign to him. What does he need that I don't buy?

I say, "A credit card. Cash. Just in case."

Six decades separate my father from Aaron. We both want him to believe it's a different century than the one that molded us. Yet even here in the suburbs, a boy of mixed race—an octoroon, by the old system—needs to look up from the phone more often, see what's coming.

My father pockets his wallet. "Keep it," he says to Aaron.

The bill, browned by age, trembles in Aaron's hand. "For real?" He looks at his grandfather, who nods again. Now, ankles creaking, we follow Aaron to his room, where he seeks among the relics of eleven years a home for this bill, unspent for fifty years.

I stop outside the bedroom. I don't want to know where Aaron keeps the bill. Its powers were always too many for me to handle. I would have tossed it away on the first bar tab, eager to prove its worth.

A father-son story that spans four generations in which so much has changed and so much has not. The story's simple gift binds the generations together, as does the complex and unspoken-as-of-yet message for the child. The story builds on the contrasts between youth and age, innocence and experience, old technology and new. No preaching, just simple wisdom and the narrator's acknowledgment that son and grandfather have just stepped away from his world a moment.

Waiting for the Big Shot

Two friends sit at a restaurant table, drinking, awaiting the arrival of an important person who has promised to change their lives. Give these friends names. Names that we won't soon forget. Describe the two of them in your notebook. Perhaps one distinguishing physical detail for each. They pass the time and relieve their anxiety with conversation. Perhaps they speculate about what change will follow the important person's revelation. What else might they talk about? Redemption? Luck? Patience? As they chat they keep looking at the entrance for the important person, whom they aren't sure they would even recognize. But the important person would recognize them, right? They imagine their new and improved lives, become quite buoyant. The waiter arrives and tells them that the important person cannot keep the appointment and has rescheduled for tomorrow at the same time. Isn't that the way with important people? Tomorrow it is, then, one of the friends says. We've waited this long, what's one more day? The other friend says the waiter has delivered this same message before. What will your characters do?

Howe's third variation is *Snap-Shot* or *Single Frame*. There is *no depicted event or incident*, only an *interior monologue* or a *flow of memory*. "A voice speaks, as it were, into the air. A mind is revealed in cross-section—and the cut is rapid." Howe considers this the hardest variation and cites the pitfalls of repetition and the sameness of a single voice. Here's a story of a baker by Brenda Miller.

AN EARLIER LIFE

In an earlier life I was a baker, in a bakery on a cobblestoned street. I woke early, in the dark, to do my work. Before the birds. Before the music of the world commenced. In the quiet, I brought something to life. I proofed yeast in large bowls, or I coddled the sourdough mother, urging it to grow. I heard only the scrape of my spoon; I smelled only yeast and flour, honey and egg. My wrists were strong. My back, strong. I knocked a Morse code on the undersides of loaves to test if they were done. Children pressed their noses to the glass, begged for small morsels to fill their mouths. I made special loaves for them, swirled in cinnamon and sugar. It was my only kindness.

Work is always interesting to read about. There are the mysteries of the workplace, the jargon, the hierarchy, the rituals, the craft, and so on. We spend most of our waking lives at work, spend more time with our coworkers than with our families. Our jobs define us to ourselves and to the world. Our self-esteem depends on our work status. Unemployment or retirement can be devastating. Here that earlier vocation is evoked, a life of vigorous industry and rationed kindness. The daily miracle of the loaves. Brenda's story employs all five senses, is dense and bittersweet, nostalgic but not sentimental.

Cheese!

When Howe uses the terms *Snap-Shot* and *Single Frame* we naturally think of photographs. With photography and the flow of memory in mind, try the following. Your narrator describes a photograph he or she is looking at, one that holds a powerful emotional charge for her. The description leads to the memory, and the memory leads to the revelation of the narrator's character. Maybe this is a photo taken on a day of great promise—a wedding, for example, or the baptism of a child—a day of joy, hope, and optimism, the very day when everything in the narrator's life fell apart. What happened?

> To survive,
> you must tell stories.
>
> —*Umberto Eco*

Confessions

Let's stick with *Snap-Shot* and *monologue*, but change it from *interior* to *dramatic*. The listener is present to the speaker, but remains unseen by the reader (unless the speaker wants us to see the listener). Try these:

- Your character is in the confessional booth at church. The screen slides open. The story begins, "Bless me, Father, for I have sinned." And the confession ensues. Know your character—his age, his temperament, his name, his values—before you proceed. And have him examine his conscience before he begins.

- You're a priest and you have just listened to the confession of another priest who has confessed to the sexual assault of a child. According to the inviolable seal of confession, you cannot divulge a word of what you've heard unless you are given permission by the penitent, which you are not. You speak to yourself or to your God or, in defiance, to whom else?

- Your character is at the therapist's. Why? Dr. Harrison-Rowan asks your character (off the page), "What does being weak mean to you?" Your character answers.

- You might consider a blog post or the confession of a crime to a police officer or a bio on a dating website as starting points for the single-frame short-short story.

- Your son has died. You have no other family. You need to tell the story for so many reasons, to purge yourself, to immortalize your son, to make sense of the obscenity, but no one will listen. That night you are home alone with your beloved dog. And you tell the little dog the whole story.

Howe's next category is the short-short that is like a *fable*. We recall Aesop, of course, and the definition of a fable: short, allegorical, moralistic, and featuring animals with human characteristics. We move past realism into the fabulous, strange, and spooky. So maybe Howe is talking about fantasy, yarns, ghost stories, and tales, not just fable. He cites Kafka's "First Sorrow" as an example, and this story of a trapeze artist has no allegorical animals in it. So let's call this category *Fantasy*. This mock-biblical short-short by David Reich will qualify.

THE LAST CREW CUT

1

Harry had a crew cut and his dog wouldn't bark.

Woe unto Harry!

But that comes later.

2

Each gray bristle of Harry's crew cut stood erect like a soldier at attention and like a blade of grass on a well-trimmed lawn.

And each gray bristle reached unto heaven with a height of thirty millimeters.

And to preserve it for the generations, Harry commanded mechanical drawings of the crew cut in all its cold precision. And when men ceased wearing crew cuts, Harry rejoiced in his heart of hearts; for he secretly wished to have the last crew cut remaining in the land.

But Harry's crew cut availed him not, for Harry had a dog that darkened his days and turned his stomach sour.

For it was a goodly Danish dog, and of wondrous girth and height, and yet it would not utter sound, and its tongue did cleave to the roof of its mouth.

And Harry in his shame kept the dog inside and did not take it out for walks, but taught it to use the toilet bowl, even to back up like a trailer truck and do its business in the toilet bowl. And when the dog finished, it would leap up and take the chain in its teeth, and lo! the toilet flushed.

And Harry in his shame sought the help of sages and men of learning. And he held consultation with great trainers of dogs; but the consultations availed him not.

And Harry cursed the Lord with weighty accusations.

And the Lord said, Who is Harry that he curses me?

And the Lord caused Harry's crew cut to bark, and Harry was ashamed.

Now Harry worked among the moneylenders in a great bank in the City, and when his crew cut barked, he feared sorely for his job.

But Harry's wife said unto him, Leash up the dog and take it with you, and the people will think it is the dog that is barking.

And Harry did as she said; but when he arrived at the door of the bank, the man that stood guard there and was Harry's friend said unto him, Harry, you are welcome, but the beast is not.

And while Harry was reasoning with his friend, the dog escaped and ran wild in the streets, and Harry's crew cut barked in the presence of his friend.

And the friend said unto Harry, Do not mock me, for I will slay you. Then the friend drew his .38.

And Harry was sore afraid and fled. And he ran wild in the streets, even as his dog ran wild, and the children of the City reviled him with jeers and stoned him and pelted him with garbage from the streets.

And the newsboys of the City broadcast tidings of a barking crew cut loosed upon the land.

And a minister of God saw Harry and said unto him, Happy is the man whom the Lord correcteth.

But Harry did not pay him heed, but continued to run wild.

But at nightfall Harry returned unto his house, and behold! his wife was gone.

And a neighbor came in unto him and said, When your wife heard of your disgrace she fell into a swoon and died.

And Harry rent his clothes and put on sackcloth with ashes and fell upon his knees and prayed to God and said, I do not ask great things, but only that my dog return.

And the Lord replied unto Harry and said, He who curses God enjoys not God's favor.

And Harry remained inside the house for forty days, until there was no food to eat, and then he sought the aid of the Welfare Department; for Harry could not go out and work inasmuch as his crew cut persisted in barking.

And the lords of Welfare came, and they searched Harry's crew cut for tiny hidden sound devices, but their search availed them not.

And they called in wise men and men of science to investigate the crew cut, and the wise men said unto the lords of Welfare, Surely it is some ventriloquist trick.

And the lords of Welfare said unto Harry, Therefore will we pay you nothing.

But in the Post Office of that time there ruled a crafty prince who heard of Harry's misfortune and said unto himself, If God has given Harry the bark of a dog, then perhaps He also gave him the nose of a dog; and if that be so, we can set him to work inspecting parcels, to determine whether evil things be contained therein.

So the prince took Harry to the great Post Office of the City and set him to work there. And Harry grew famous as a worker with parcels, and his name was much set by, for the people said, If you doubt what there be in a certain parcel, then bring it unto Harry.

And by night, certain daughters of the land came in unto Harry and gave him consolation, wherefore it was said, Great good has come out of great misfortune.

But it came to pass after several years that the Lord remembered Harry, and it did not please the Lord that Harry had waxed strong among the people. And the Lord said, Woe is Harry, for he is an abomination.

And when Harry was in the Post Office, at work among the parcels, the Lord overthrew the place and utterly destroyed it. And the columns and the walls did crumble, and hundreds, even thousands, were crushed to death.

And the Lord looked on His work, and He was satisfied.

Speak!

In the last exercises, you may have noticed that I cribbed the plot of the dead son from Chekhov's story "Misery," and substituted a dog for a mare. So let's stick with the dog for now and write a flash fable. We'll go easy on the allegory. If Jack London and William Maxwell can get the reader into the mind of a dog, so can we. Why don't you decide on the breed of your dog, and since we're talking fable here, don't necessarily limit yourself to American Kennel Club breeds. And give the dog a name. And trouble. The dog is lost. The dog is chained to a stake. The dog has been abandoned. The dog listens to a woeful story from its bereft owner and doesn't know how to alleviate the friend's pain. And the moral of the fable is . . . ?

I have a copy of the 1948 second edition of *Writers: Try Short Shorts!* by Mildred I. Reid and Delmar E. Bordeaux, published by Bellevue Books, Rockford, Illinois. Mildred got her handsome photo on the back of the dust jacket. Delmar did not. We learn that Mildred conducted writing classes at her studio in the Chicago Loop and at her writing colony in the New Hampshire mountains. We learn nothing about Delmar. But a quick look on Amazon reveals that our man Delmar is the sole author of *Cosmetic Electrolysis and the Removal of Superfluous Hair*, which sounds like a delightful title for a very short story. Amazon will let you have the book for $299.99, not eligible for Prime. We also learn that Delmar's middle name is Emil.

Eight Stories

Mildred and Delmar list eight types of short-shorts, and perhaps we can try to write one of each:

1. The Complication Short-Short. The authors cite O. Henry as a source for this type of story and note that it achieves its effect with the "well-known 'trick ending.'" Consider Jim Thompson's definition of a plot: Things are not as they seem. A young woman is rescued by a motorist when her car breaks down on a lonely stretch of highway. Once inside the

man's car, things get creepy. His conversation is inappropriate, his behavior menacing. Turn the tables if you can.

2. The Character Short-Short. The authors distinguish between two versions: *Utter Consistency* (of character) and *Apparent Inconsistency*, which portrays two opposing impressions of a character, the latter impression the true one. So let's take Delmar's book as a prompt. An electrologist in Natchitoches, Louisiana, consults with an attractive young writer from Chicago, in town visiting her cousins. She has unwanted facial hair she'd like removed. Let's say this is 1940 or so. What does his office look like? He tells her he does a little writing himself. She's unimpressed. Maybe he lies and says he's Kate Chopin's grandson. He considers his patient's aloof demeanor to be a result of her embarrassing appearance. After the procedure, which proves mostly successful, his impression of her changes. How? She looks in the mirror and says . . .

3. The Decision Short-Short. Just like it sounds. A character must choose between two suitors, between living or dying, between thinking of himself or others, between a job and a loved one, between two loyalties. So today you've decided to change your life. Your job is deadening and humiliating. How? You don't want to wake up at sixty and feel the regret of not having followed your dreams. Of not having at least taken a chance. You'll take care of the wife and kids somehow. You're going to do it—you're going to write. You call your wife on the cell, look up, and see your boss headed your way with that sour look on his bloated face. Your wife says, Hi, hon. Continue.

4. The Reconciliation-Alienation Short-Short. Briefly, in the first version, a character is about to be alienated from a

loved one, but is reconciled by his observation of the other's behavior. In the second, a character is alienated from the other by the revelation of some unsavory behavior. Let's try both at once: She's here in the lobby of the Hotel Aurora to meet Mr. X., a man she first met on thatsamore.com and with whom she has conducted a considerable and intriguing correspondence. She has situated herself at a secluded table for two with a view of the clock tower beneath which they have agreed to meet at just this moment. The man standing there does not look like the picture of Mr. X. she's seen on the computer. She'll wait. And watch. What she sees makes up her mind. Write the short-short where they meet. The short-short where they don't.

5. The Psychological Short-Short, which our authors define as a character in the grips of an overpowering illusion, which we might think of as a delusion. Your central character believes that his wife has been replaced by an imposter who appears identical, but isn't the same person. They are both at the breakfast table.

6. The Dilemma Short-Short. I quote: ". . . the protagonist . . . involves himself in a situation impossible to explain—and this at a time when a satisfactory explanation is absolutely necessary to his future well-being." Not sure I catch the authors' drift, but maybe this will fit the bill. Write this short-short: "Pulling the Plug on Mom." Consider the ethical dilemma, the relationship of the child to the ailing mom, Mom's physical and mental condition. And, of course, the powerful and grinding emotions!

7. The Parallel-Action Short-Short. O. Henry again. Think "The Gift of the Magi." A character sets out to deceive another

person, while the other person sets out to deceive the first. The deception is not necessarily malicious. Maybe something like this. A husband is keeping quiet about his dire medical prognosis so as not to spoil his and his wife's fiftieth anniversary. A week before the anniversary, she presents him with a gift: tickets for a six-month-long world cruise. Write the scene where he opens the card.

8. The Identity Short-Short depends for its effect on the revelation of the identity of a person or a thing that has decisively affected the action of the story. Maupassant's "The Diamond Necklace"* is cited as an example. Your character is adopted and has been searching for her biological parents for years. When she finally gets to meet her father, he is a man she knows all too well.

* Just to be clear, Maupassant's story and those by O. Henry cited here are not what we are calling very short stories.

The Lure of Stories

*You can't visit readers where you think they are. You have
to invite them home to where you are and try to lure them
into your universe. That's the art of storytelling.*

—Jo Nesbø

Before we discuss the qualities of a good short-short story,
let's think about the basic elements of a short-short story.
We need:

A beginning, middle, and end, but not necessarily in that
order. Let's call this the narrative structure. Narrative structure is the matrix (from the Latin for *womb*) in which the plot
is nurtured and developed. If plot is the causal shape of the
story, narrative structure is the chronological and the architectural. The beginnings may be and often are abrupt—you
don't have time to go somewhere; you're already there, in the
middle of things. The endings are also sudden. They suggest
rather than conclude or offer insight. By way of example, here's
a story by Rachel Luria that seems to begin at the end and lets
us imagine the beginning. It was inspired, by the way, by a
1950s-vintage ad for Solfera tablets, which featured a woman

blotting her tears and the headline "PERIOD DELAYED? . . .
Don't Worry!"

THE CHANGE

Shelia thought she'd finally got her miracle. A baby at
fifty-five. But Dr. Hero said her period wasn't delayed, it
was done for. Menopause, she said, emphasis on pause as
if to tell Shelia to stop hoping, stop trying, stop living altogether. *What will I tell Bill?* she wondered. *He'll be so smug
about it all.*

Shelia clutched her paper nightie closed at the neck.
The exam table stuck to her sweaty thighs and she peeled
herself off it one leg at a time. The change, she thought. The
change had come. "So there's nothing left?" she asked. "I'm
all dried up."

"Not my words," said Dr. Hero.

There was a poster of a woman's insides on the wall and
a plastic uterus on a shelf beside it. Curled up inside the
plastic uterus was a plastic baby. Shelia tried to imagine a
baby inside her. She'd done it a million times these last few
weeks, but she couldn't now. She let the nightie drop open
and felt the A/C prickle her skin.

———

There will be no miracle for Sheila. There's only the indignity of
the paper nightie, the annoyance of the A/C, the emptiness, the
futility of the imagination, the change, and the end of hope. Not
an extra word in this story and not a word out of place. So sad and
so succinct.

A plot. No matter how luminous your prose and how fascinating your characters, if you have no plot—no narrative shape—if the characters have nothing meaningful to accomplish, the reader will put down your story. The longer your story, the more dependent on plot you are. And the basic plot of every story is this: a central character wants something intensely, goes after it despite opposition, and as a result of a struggle comes to a win or a loss. In very short stories, the plot may be elliptical, that is, missing, off the page, implied rather than expressed. But you need to know that plot yourself so you can leave it out while letting it cast its light on the narrative. And here's an elliptical plot in a story by Brenda Miller about a Greek Island.

CRUSH

Years ago, on the island of Santorini, I walked the village at sunrise, gazing at vineyards that grow differently there— close to the ground, like mounded beans, rather than the upright regiments I knew in California. In Greece, the grapes sprawl in leisure, indifferent to the future. Or not indifferent, but plump with it, glad to be turned to a greater purpose. I always want to be there, in that village at dawn; I want to be those grapes beholden to the wine, born to a pleasure that comes only after the crush.

Who I am and who I was. Now and then. Here and there. Only the hint of trouble in those upright regiments. Here we have

Greece, where Western culture began, and California, where it is headed. Here is a world in which the future (libation) determines the past (cultivation). And, of course, it's all about place, which brings us to:

A setting: because nothing happens nowhere, and you can't move the world if you have no place to set your lever. The setting of a story colors the people and events in the story and shapes what happens. Place connects characters to a collective and a personal past, and so place is the emotional center of story. And by *place*, I don't simply mean *location*. A location is a dot on a map, a set of coordinates. Place is location with narrative, with memory and imagination, with a history. Here's a brilliant very short and quite alarming story that's also a song by Rennie Sparks, one half of the Handsome Family, along with her husband, Brett.

LAKE GENEVA

You are crouched before the fire in a state park by the highway and through the heavy pine trees ten-ton trucks go groaning by. Like the screams of your Aunt Barbara who went crazy in the '70's, wrote poems to Jimmy Carter, but forgot to feed her kids. But, it's the first time you're together since he got out of the hospital. Raccoons in the darkness drag off your hot dog buns. But, you're happy just to lie there in a plastic tent from Walmart like sticks and fallen dead leaves to feed the fire of the world. Because which is more important, to comfort an old woman or see visions of the heavens in the stumps of fallen trees? Albert Einstein trembled when he saw that time was water, seeping through the rafters to put out this burning world. Next morning you're at Waffle House. Toast and eggs and hash browns. Truckers chain-smoke Camels over plastic cups of juice. And you remember how he cried when they strapped him to the stretcher, convinced his arms were burning with electricity from heaven. You remember how he told you that black holes were like Jesus. And the crucifix was a battery that filled the air with fire.

There is always a strong sense of place in Rennie's narratives. Here, Big Foot State Park in Lake Geneva, Wisconsin. Big trouble: insanity. Not once but twice. A campground, not in the wilderness, but by the highway. We'll see those truckers again in the morning. And that startling metaphor: time as water dousing our lives. A fiercely condensed one-page novel. An example of a short-short that compresses time, what Irving Howe called One Thrust of Incident. There is more information implied here than stated. Years of pain and fear and loneliness.

You need an evocative mood and you need vivid and significant, resonant, and unforgettable images (more on images in a moment). And "Lake Geneva" has both. In fact, Rennie uses the images to create the mood. She doesn't tell us how to feel; she presents the images and we respond: Walmart and Waffle House: we know what side of town we're on; chain-smoking truckers, plastic cups of juice, the plastic tent, dead leaves, fallen trees, discarded hot dog buns, nothing we haven't experienced in our own lives, but the accumulation of details adds up to sadness, and to that add your dear friend screaming as he's tied to a stretcher, and we're nearing desperation. And that galvanic crucifix, igniting the air with fire! Here's Rennie again, attending to those details, summoning the mood.

CATHEDRALS

The cathedral in Cologne looks like a spaceship, like the hand of God falling from the sky. A thousand stone-carved saints hang like icicles, but icicles don't take a thousand years to die. And everyone who ever worked on this cathedral or even spent a moment walking by, every one of us is swept away like bread crumbs. What comfort does it bring, soaring towers left behind? There's a fiberglass castle in Wisconsin where kids race go-carts around a moat. Once we went up there in December when every waterslide and fudge shop was closed. Hoping to feel love under the icicles. All we did was drink in an empty bar. But, stumbling drunk, we crawled back to our motel room and I fell against you and felt your beating heart. Snow was slowly falling on the ice machine and the moon shone hazy through the pines. But, there were lounge chairs thrown into the empty pool and a dog chained to a tree barking at the sky.

Note the movement from the sublime to the derelict. The contrast between then and now, granite and fiberglass, spaceships and go-carts, the falling hand of God and the falling snow, the cathedral and the empty, littered pool, art and life. Where do we find our comfort? Our solace? In grand monuments to gods or in the arms of lovers? Mutability—swept way like bread crumbs.

You can listen to "Cathedrals" on the Handsome Family album *Through the Trees*.

Vivid character(s), at least one of whom we can care about. This would seem to go without saying. Character is the heart of fiction. All stories are about people. People in trouble. We read stories for the people who inhabit them because we read to find out about ourselves, to learn something about the human condition. When we remember the stories we love, we remember the characters in them. Successful characters tend to be independent, eccentric, perhaps quirky. They don't always do what they are supposed to do. That's why we care about them. They aren't types or clichés; they are unique individuals, unlike anyone we've ever met. And characters are likely to be in pain, in doubt, in love, and in misery. E. M. Forster described characters as round (as in well-rounded) or flat (as in one-dimensional). And the test of a round character is that she can surprise us in a convincing way. A flat character in his purest form, according to Forster, is "constructed round a single idea or quality." Remember that every character has attitude, memories, and secrets, has had traumas in her life, has friends and enemies, aspirations and regrets. Every character feels a yearning and may experience pain or exaltation. You won't, however, have the time to render your characters in very much detail when you're writing the short-short, and you won't have the space for more than one or two characters.

Here's a character who leaps off the page in a story by David Norman, which was inspired by something Bob Dylan said: "I wake and I'm one person, and when I go to sleep I know for certain I'm somebody else."

THE DOG LOVERS

On the Island, I dream I'm a conquistador straight out of one of my father's books. Not Cabeza de Vaca, but his cowardly old friend, Lope de Oviedo. I'm Lope de Oviedo, I tell myself, and in my dream I wake to see Cabeza de Vaca paddling across the bay.

He comes ashore and asks if I'm ready to escape with him back to Pánuco, civilization. His lips tremble as he speaks. Sand and white sea foam hang in his beard. I roll over on my side and shake my head and say, "It's not yet time for me, friend."

My muscles ache from the sickness that has invaded the Island. De Vaca doesn't stay long. He asks me how my captors are treating me and if my health has gotten any better. "No better, no worse," I say. When he leaves, I scavenge for crabs, oysters, fish. For their women I will carry bundled roots on my back and tread barefoot across oyster shells.

At night, I'm always limping just beyond the edge of their campfire. They never welcome me into their circle. I'm nothing more than a shadow of these people the Spaniards call the Dog Lovers. Spying, loping, starved, beaten with sticks, I am my father's least loved character.

The sea is a fire at my back. At dawn the sun bleeds out of the gulf, and the surf leaps and snaps and howls so loud I turn around, thinking it's them, the Dog Lovers. They'll blame me for this sickness, and if I can't cure them, they'll slaughter me. I'll become another victim, buried, unburied, they'll eat my flesh. All night I hear the horrible sound of their ritual weeping.

Often I'm performing some task for their women. Weaving baskets. Sharpening spears. Making a fire. Last night, one of their elders struck me across the head and laughed. She told me to dig a hole and spread her hands to show me how deep. Another woman said what goes in won't come out until we're finished with the others.

I understand their language, but I can't speak it. So I show them how I can't dig unless they let me eat the food I've gathered. I lift my arms, my withered arms, all sinew and bone.

They leave me, and I grow angry. I try to dig, but the sand collapses around my fists. The bottom of the hole rises like the bottom of an hourglass. My fingers throb. Slowly the sand turns to a wet mud that smells like rotting fish. I raise my head, I glance at the moon, the shimmering sea. I should have left with my friend. He won't come back for me.

With the moon and stars burning above, I scratch my message in the sand: Here lies Lope de Oviedo, old coward, gentleman, friend. With the sea and the Dog Lovers wailing, I lower my body into my pit of sand.

———————

Historical flash. Álvar Núñez Cabeza de Vaca was a Spanish explorer, a survivor of the 1527 Narváez expedition. He traveled the American Southwest and Mexico and wrote an account of his observations. Lope de Oviedo accompanied Cabeza to Mexico. They parted ways at Matagorda Bay, and Oviedo was never heard from again. He did not produce a written record of his experiences among the Karankawa Indians until now, we might say, through the dream of the author's son.

A theme. A story has to be about something, and that something ought to be significant. What is it that you have to say about that something? *Subject* is what the story is about. *Theme* is what about what the story's about. It's the abstraction made flesh. The idea treated by action or by discourse or by both. Not loneliness, in other words, but what you have to say about that loneliness. Theme is where the writing meets the world. Theme is part of what attracts you to your material, if you're writing about what's important to you and about what you don't understand. Theme is why the story is worth telling. It's why you care, and why your readers will. And it emanates from character, not plot. And here's a theme-driven short-short story by Cynthia Chinelly that honors both words and silence, what is said and what is withheld, what is fragile and what is broken, what is spoken and what is heard, what is lost and what can be saved.

A SIGNIFICANT WEATHER
EVENT OF MY CHILDHOOD

APRIL 11, 1965—THE PALM SUNDAY TORNADOES

I was five and knew even then that this moment would come.

The ringer on the wall phone in the kitchen was broken. Instead, the phone vibrated impatiently. I lay on my stomach across the floor, cool ceramic tile the color of fresh snow. My parents were in their bedroom upstairs, their voices small at first, hearts of syllables whirling through heating ducts.

I played with my mother's Lark cigarettes, examining them with a magnifying glass, the red-lettered "LARK" stamped just below the filter. Each time she finished the last puff, I imagined the letters curling in her lungs, rearranging themselves until my father's name, Karl, billowed in her blood, believed that as long as she kept smoking, she could never leave him, the gasp of his name settling in the back of her throat.

Scraps of light scalded the ceiling above me.

There was the blue echo of a water glass breaking. A shallow scream. I pinched off the filter of a cigarette, let it roll across the tiles. His voice was sober, flat like a footprint. I peeled the paper away from the tobacco, brown flecks flying with even the lightest breath.

And then her voice all electric and wild—But it's not my heart.

And, yes, the wall phone in the kitchen was vibrating, a wrong number, a boy just five himself, six hundred miles west of me, his church clothes barely loosened, dialing who he thought was his grandmother to tell what he saw. The green sky, the wall of clouds, the dishrag rain. And then the sound, a little at first like the deepening rush of bathwater, and then a metal roar leaning into his ears, against his chest, as he watched his mother running from a neighbor's porch, the mouth of her thin dress giving in to the wind, her waist-length hair all frothy and black. And how he held his breath the whole time, counting seconds or was it the number of heartbeats, until finally when the screen door swung wide and she was ten counts away, all of it—the sickly light, the horn of wind, the blur of dust and rain—took her in a flash-lit moment so brief his breath knocked free.

And I heard it above me, my mother's desperate loveliness blowing through the doors and windows, the darkness beneath her, a cushion of crushed reeds. I climbed up the red-lacquered stool to the phone, held it in two hands. Close.

An embrace that took all of my heart.

From the understated title to the heroic and heartbreaking last line, from the whirling hearts to the pounding hearts, from the still small voices to the voice wild and electric, from the robust verbs and the brilliant flights of synesthesia—the blue echo and the scraps of scalding light—to the litany of all that is broken—the phone, the glass, the cigarette, the family, the heart, and the future—this is a lesson in telling a story with artful compression and soaring lyricism.

Images. Stories, like dreams, exist in images. Not ideas. They are sensual. Like dreams, fiction communicates in visual images because, for most of us, vision is our primary vehicle for understanding the world. Why images? To involve you in the story, to engage your narrative imagination. To affect your emotions. Images are more vivid and more emotionally powerful than abstractions. In dreams, images and words are significantly separate. "Seeing comes before words," John Berger says.

Here's what some other noted thinkers have had to say.

- "In a way, nobody sees a flower, really, it is so small, we haven't the time—and to see takes time. Like to have a friend takes time." Georgia O'Keeffe

- "I very rarely think in words at all. A thought comes, and I may try to express it in words afterwards." And this: "The words or the language, as they are written or spoken, do not seem to play any role in my mechanism of thought. The entities, which seem to serve as elements in thought, are certain signs and more or less clear images which can be 'voluntarily' reproduced and combined." Albert Einstein

- "I think in pictures. Words are like a second language to me. I translate both spoken and written words into full-color movies, complete with sound, which run like a VCR tape in my head. When somebody speaks to me, his words are instantly translated into pictures." Temple Grandin

Writing stories, and reading them, can teach us how to see O'Keeffe's flowers. How to look closely, how to pay attention. Maybe we should all cultivate our visual thinking. Vision is the most sophisticated and highly developed of our five-plus senses, and our brains have become extremely powerful tools for processing and storing concrete visual images. This imag-

ery is the real language of the brain, not abstract construc-
tions like words.

If I ask you to think of your bedroom, what comes to your
mind is the picture of the bedroom, not the words that describe
it. If I ask you to think of, or remember, your grandmother,
you see her, you see the color of her hair and the glasses on her
face. Pictures are how our minds talk to us. Dreams are a daily
way that we think visually. Words are relatively unimportant
and in some cases not there at all. Write out your dreams in
the morning. Attend especially to your visual images. What
were those seven blue cats doing there? Why was Noel Paradise wheeling a green mattress through busy traffic outside the
bar you were drinking at with three intimate friends whom
you don't really know?

Memories are another daily, almost constant, way that we
think visually. As I suggested above. Recall where you were
when you heard about the World Trade Center 9/11 bombings,
and you see where you were and what you did when you understood the horror.

A picture is worth a thousand words. Draw or sketch in your
notebook. Sketch to help you remember. Draw to reinforce the
images you're looking at. The hotel room you're sitting in could
be the hotel room your character, a woman running for her life,
is sitting in. Drawing the room, no matter how simply, will help
you remember all of the details of the room not on the page.
Your notebook could, and maybe should, be filled with sketches
as well as words.

Here's a very short story by Ruthann Ward that attends brilliantly
to subtle visual images.

WELL CUT

"Have a tissue," I say, working the bunch from my purse. The young woman in the gold trench coat smiles, nods toward the empty chair. I wonder at the ease with which she feels familiar, but people in distress do presumptuous things. She eyes her cell phone as if it were alive.

"I can't believe this," she says, tugging gingerly at the sleeve of her coat. I had been watching her for some time, feeling voyeuristic, but not enough to stop. Saw the distress, but couldn't get past the coat. Beautifully cut. Much better than her outfit. I would have worn it with the collar up.

"Man trouble?"

"It shows?"

Leaking from every pore.

She wipes her eyes with her sleeve, catches herself, then readjusts the cuff with reverence.

This coat's a gift. Couture. Hand stitching. And the color. I had similar coats, but never in such a color. Sunflowers. The color of sunflowers. Mine were beige. This man was trying to make her into something else, a younger, exciting version of someone else.

"This happened once before. His wife found out." Her eyes wander from side to side with the memory, then settle on me. "But he came back. You know how that goes," she says.

More than you know.

"This is different. He wants to give her another chance," she says, emphasizing each pronoun. "They actually had new rings made in Florence, I mean, Firenze."

Good work. This girl's trying. I fold my hands deeper into my lap.

"He wears it . . . I should have known. It's beautiful. Says he's doing the mature thing. What he really means is the convenient thing. I'm not convenient." She dabs her sleeve with a napkin, trying to preserve something wonderful, something sacred.

"Don't worry about your sleeve. Tears don't stain," I say. "History does." I surprise myself, and look directly into her eyes, this girl who merited such a beautifully hued coat.

"You sound like him." She clears her throat. "Wait, that call saying he wasn't coming here. It was from his landline," she says, grabbing her phone, checking the log. "He never does that . . . uses his cell. Safer . . . and he was talking . . . sort of like . . . a speech?" Her head bobs on a slender unlined neck.

"Rehearsed?"

She bites the inside of her cheek. "Like someone was listening."

"You were."

"No, not me. Her." Her speech quickens, she becomes as lively as her coat. "Women do that all the time. The man calls, the wife listens. We think that makes them honest. But we both know that it doesn't."

No, that one doesn't.

"That's it. He'll call me later . . ." She plants both hands on the table. Triumphant. "He's keeping me."

Suddenly I feel tired and heavy for both of us. Common, diminished. No, not at all the plan.

I lift my left hand. All the way from Firenze.

Here our narrator, a therapist, listens to an all-too-familiar story, one she has lived through herself. She is alert to the telling details of body language and to the nuances of speech. She has earned our trust. And at the end of her story she has changed even if her client has not, even if the client has rejected a chance, maybe her last, for change in favor of being a kept woman. Security or freedom. You get to choose.

> Your intuition knows what to write, so get out of the way.
>
> —*Ray Bradbury*

Words. Words are all we have, Samuel Beckett reminded us. Every character we animate, every room we construct, every town we build, all of it we do with words. With words we cast our spells. In a letter to Balzac, Stendhal wrote, "Often I ponder a quarter of an hour whether to place an adjective before or after its noun. [He was writing in French, of course.] I seek (1) to be truthful, (2) clear in my accounts of what happens in a human heart." That's how important language is, or ought to be, to a fiction writer. Flaubert's protégé Maupassant wrote, "Whatever you want to say, there is only one word to express it, one verb to set it in motion, and only one adjective to describe it." Susan Bell, in her marvelous book *The Artful Edit*, contends that "language determines that transcendent aspect of the writer's work: her unique style, her voice." She has a checklist of editing suggestions: keep language fresh; keep it precise and concise; keep it active; and keep it real. In a letter to Joseph Conrad, Ford Madox Ford addressed language: "We used to say that a passage of good style began with a fresh, usual word, and continued with fresh, usual words to the end: there was nothing more to it." The fresh, usual word. Not the esoteric word, but the word you've heard before but never in quite this way or have never seen in this position in the sentence. Hart Day Leavitt put it like this: "It is not unusual words that count but unusual combinations of usual words."

> Style is the difference between a circle and the way you draw it.
> —*Pablo Picasso*

And here's a story, a portrait of the artist as a young woman, that honors the power and the crucial importance of words and is all about opening up a brave new world. Our narrator defines her world by writing it, defies her mother by appropriating her mother's ritual. The short-short story is by Julie Marie Wade, and it's mighty like a rose.

PORTRAIT OF THE CHILD AFTER THE FALL

This time, the garden was empty. The mother had gone to the grandmother's house for her customary afternoon tea. The child had not been invited. In fact, they were not speaking at the moment due to an unfortunate incident involving the child's diary & the mother's curiosity. The child had characterized this incident as *trespass*. The mother had declared it *treason*. "Who gave you permission," the mother inquired, "to write such things about me?" The child returned the mother's gaze, undaunted. "This is my story, not yours, & I shall write whatever I please." As a consequence of her *smart mouth*, the child was forcefully withdrawn to the powder room. "Are you trying to make me angry? Is that your intention?" the mother had asked, moistening a bar of soap. "That's poison, you know," the child remarked, pointing to the foaming IVORY. "You have no respect for other people's feelings," the mother proclaimed. "*You* have no respect for other people's *privacy*," the child countered. And so the mother bent the child's head over the sink & broke the soap into wafer-sized pieces. "Hold this in your teeth," she commanded, & when the child refused, the mother clasped her jaw & piled from her tongue to the roof of her mouth an assortment of the white soap-tiles. "I want you to hold them there & think about what you've done, & when you're ready to apologize, you may spit them out." The child held the soap-tiles a long time in her mouth as the tears stormed her cheeks & streamed over the crest of her chin. But when at last she relented, there was no apology, only silence aggravated by avoidance & the torching of her journals, page by page, over a scalloped dish with a book of matches. Now the mother was away, & the child wandered the length of the property— there among the ferns, beneath the dogwood, to the corner of the yard where she imagined a stranger's surveillance through the lattice of the fence & the overarching lilacs. She took off her shirt, despite the fact she was flat as a stone, her nipples tiny & pink & hard—*indignant*. She wanted to touch herself lower in the body, but she didn't know how, & she was frightened of the first hairs that seemed to signal witchcraft or betrayal of some secret ordinance. The child turned her attention instead to the roses, which were just beginning to spread their petals in the afternoon sun. The mother loved these roses, fed & watered them, managed their soil, supervised their blooms. It was possible the child was jealous of these flowers. It was also possible that she only wanted revenge. The child had always applauded the mother's green thumb, though she did not apprentice herself to the art of cultivation. One by one, she decapitated them, piling each red petal onto her tongue. Slowly, she severed them, then wantonly chewed & swallowed.

A voice. You write the story, but a narrator, whom you create, tells it. Who is telling the story and how is she telling it? And what is the sound of her voice? That narrator may or may not be a character in the story. Choosing a narrator is a matter of point of view: Where do we stand to view the events or event of the story; into whose consciousness, if any, do we delve? Point of view deserves its own chapter, so that's where we're going next.

Points of View

The choice of point-of-view will largely determine all other choices with regards to style, diction, characteristic speed of sentences and so on. What the writer must consider, obviously, is the extent to which point-of-view, and all that follow from it, comments on the characters, actions, and ideas.

—John Gardner

YOU WRITE the story, but a narrator, a persona, tells it. Your choice of narrator is a question of POV. Who is speaking and how? Through whose consciousness is the story understood? This is how both the reader and the writer come to understand the story.

- **First Person:** *I have a wandering eye, not in the* forbidden fruit *sense of the word, but in the less familiar and less hazardous* strabismus *sense.*

- **Second Person:** *To conceal the offending abnormality from the distressed gazes of fragile strangers, you wear a tinted right lens on your eyeglasses.*

- **Third Person:** *He and his friend Otto occupy a corner table, facing the entrance, at the House of Wheat and Water restaurant in Normal.*

More important than person (first, second, or third, as above) is distance: How close are we to the hearts and minds of the characters? And to what depth do we delve? You can write a very short story in any point of view. Which POV will most effectively and efficiently address your goal and explore the values and motivations of the characters? Which POV will best answer the question *Why?*

We tell stories about ourselves in first person. So that may seem natural. But all fairy tales are in third. So that may seem authentic. Let's take a look at each of the points of view.

FIRST PERSON: The pronoun *I.* Or perhaps *we.* There are three forms:

- **The informant I:** I'm sitting at the bar, minding my own business, when this guy walks in with an iridescent green iguana wrapped around his neck and takes the stool beside mine.*

- **The reminiscent I:** It all started one miserably hot summer afternoon in Dania Beach thirty years ago. I remember it like it was yesterday. I was sitting alone in this bar when in walked this guy . . .

---

* With apologies to the late, great James Crumley, whose magnificent opening line to *The Last Good Kiss* I have messed with.

- **The unreliable I:** I knew the guy with the iguana would show up at the bar because I have this ability to know the future, and I also knew that the reptile had been a long-shoreman in Port Everglades in his last life.

And now an example of each. First from Tom DeMarchi an example of the first-person informant, a narrator who is a character telling the story as it seems to unfold.

MÖBIUS STRIPS

The doors are bolted, the windows sealed—of this I'm sure, just as I'm sure that Rosemary's lying beside me, beneath an itchy afghan in a bed I've slept in since I was eleven years old, a bed I had shipped via train from Peabody to Fresno to Miami, back to Peabody, back to my parents' aluminum-insulated ranch that's currently getting pelted with snow. Rosemary's jugular pulses in the red glow of my digital clock, and I wonder if the whistle I hear is wind blowing through a crack in the window, air through Rosemary's nostrils, or the B&M railroad chugging past the reservoir three blocks away, or if I'm dreaming of the past, of July 1979, when Mark X—what was that boy's name?—and I hiked home after swimming in the reservoir and lined the tracks with pennies, watched the 2:19 whizz past, blow-dry our hair, spit copper tears at our feet.

My father shuffles down the hallway to the front door. I picture him twisting the knob, unlocking and locking the dead bolt, traipsing from window to window, unlatching and latching.

He stops in the dining room, presses palms and forehead to glass, stares at the plowed snow barricading his driveway. He sighs at the thought of shoveling in a few hours, when his stomach will churn coffee and Cheerios. A shiver sends him back down the hall to my bedroom door, where he pauses.

My mother, a nurse, says the human brain is a series of Möbius strips lined with locked filing cabinets, that neural atrophy causes us to begin losing keys at age twenty-three. My mother says crossword puzzles, a steady diet of blueberries, long walks, needlepoint, and thick history books keep those keys jingling on our hips, keep the hallways lit. My mother posits this theory weekly, as if it just occurred to her.

I wonder if my father's standing in the hallway because he's wondering if he locked the front door. Names of old golfing buddies, where he put his glasses, his age: just some of the things my father chases down dark hallways. I wonder if he wonders if he's showing signs of Alzheimer's, like Mr. Otto, a neighbor once arrested for pissing against the wall of the 7-Eleven, and who, like my father just last week, reported his car stolen after he'd forgotten where he parked.

I wonder whether I'll remember this moment: Rosemary's pulsing jugular, B&M's fading whistle, my father frozen in the hallway, cold fingertips pressing his forehead, and me—now—disentangling myself from the afghan's itchy embrace, easing into my slippers, opening my bedroom door, startling my father into saying, "Jesus!," planting my index finger on his lips, taking his hand, leading him from window to window, door to door, jiggling door-knobs and testing locks, securing the house so both of us can sleep without any regard for the snow piling up outside.

Tom's story is a reminder that we should be writing about what keeps us up at night, what is of crucial importance in our lives. Write about what's unspeakably frightening down all our dark hallways.

Jason Skipper's short-short story is an example of a first-person reminiscent and reflective narrator. This POV has two *I*'s: a boy in the car with his dad an hour before his dad, Wrendon, revealed his illness, and the older driver who is remembering the experience and telling us the story. The dad Wrendon is, of course, the reminiscent narrator of the story he tells his son, our narrator.

GHOSTS

This was an hour before my dad brought his cancer into our lives. One hour before he reached inside the glovebox of our Dodge conversion van for the pamphlets. The ones with cartoons and words like benign, malignant, and larynx, all explained. I had just gotten my learner's permit and we were coming back from Galveston on a Thursday night in June, having just packed our twelve Igloo coolers full of the shrimp that we sold from the van outside of a flea market on weekends. We were headed to our home in

Fort Worth, where we'd unload the coolers and store them in the shed in his backyard. Driving through Huntsville, there were no lights other than ours. I was trying to keep the hood ornament lined up with the reflective white line on the side of the road, holding my foot steady to keep the speed consistent. My window was open and warm air slipped though. My dad sat in the passenger's seat, sipping a can of Schlitz and smoking a Merit. He put out the cigarette and lit another, turned down the radio and rolled up his window, something he did when he was about to talk and needed me to listen close.

He held the cigarette between his knuckles as he spoke. He said, "You see this hill we're coming up on?"

I squinted and leaned forward to see and said, "Yes."

"One night while I was making this trip by myself," he said, "right about here where we're at now, I saw your granddad's ghost sitting where I'm sitting now. As real as me beside you. Right here in this seat."

I looked at him out of the corner of my eye and said, "Yeah, right." He didn't say anything for a minute and I looked over to see he wasn't smiling or grinning. I said, "You saw Buddy?"

My dad shook his empty beer can, rolled the window down a little, and tossed it out. As he reached behind his seat to grab another from his Styrofoam cooler, he pushed the button on the glove compartment and closed it right back up. He flicked ice off the can. "I was driving," he said. "Going between eighty and ninety miles an hour, when I hear this voice. Clear as day, it says, 'Wrendon, slow the van down.' I looked over, and sure enough it was him. Do you remember those short-sleeve button-downs he wore? The way he kept his hair combed back over his head?"

Buddy had died three years before. I remembered his clothes. His white face and deep wrinkles. The peppermint smell of the Brylcreem in his hair. I felt cold and rolled up my window up so my dad's voice was clearer.

"I started to slow down," he said. "Going about sixty, coming up over this hill, when he says it again: He said, 'Wrendon, I'm not kidding. You need to slow the van down.'"

I watched the road through the windshield, imagining Buddy's voice, deep and stern. He spoke in a way where he'd never need to repeat himself. I didn't mean to slow the van down, but saw the dashes of yellow lines in the road getting clearer. We were the only car that I had seen for miles, and now in the dark surrounded by pine trees we seemed far off into nowhere. I wanted my dad to stop and laugh and say he was kidding.

"So I did it," Wrendon said. "By the time we reached the top, I was only doing twenty miles an hour. And as I came over this hill, the engine cut out completely." He took another long drink from his beer. "All I had were the head-lights and lights from the console. I looked over and Buddy was gone. I coasted over the top of this hill. And do you know what was on the other side? Have I told you this?"

I sat up in my seat to see over the hill and said, "No."

"A semi was jackknifed in the road," Wrendon said. "A big red Peterbilt, with the trailer turned over, spread out from one side of the highway to the next. A big wall."

And I saw it. A red truck with its face turned toward us, the large rectangular trailer lying across both lanes of the highway. Our van was nearly at a standstill, there in the dark. I could have counted out the black tar lines in the road, like little cracks.

My dad said, "What are you doing? Why are you going so slow?" He waved his hand in a shooing motion, saying to push forward, and with that all of what I saw was gone.

I pushed on the gas.

"I wouldn't be here tonight," my dad said, "had your granddad not appeared. I would have driven straight into that semi. It would have killed me. But it didn't. And do you know why?"

The road got smooth again, with the lines flowing beneath us. I sat back down, feeling my heart in my chest, the sweat on my hands.

"Because my dad was still with me, keeping an eye out."

Wrendon sat back in his chair for a moment, looking forward. I looked at the rearview mirror. The road was empty. The night before us hung in the sky, the large pine trees lined the road. I had stopped looking out at the ornament on the hood of the van and knew I wouldn't need to do that anymore. My arms stayed tight, and I realized Wrendon wasn't quite yet finished. I figured the hill had brought on the story, nothing more.

"I'm telling you all of this for a reason," Wrendon said. "You don't know it, but we come from a long line of ghosts. I want to tell you right now that whatever happens, I'll always be around. I still talk to your granddad sometimes. Not just at his gravesite, but sometimes in my prayers. You should feel free to do that too, someday, with me. Don't feel foolish. I ask him questions, and I get answers. Sometimes I do it because I miss him, and I know that he'll be listening.

I do it so he knows that I haven't and won't forget him. And I do it so he knows that somewhere he's still alive."

———————————

Here we listen to Wrendon's preface to his grim revelation, a story that unites our narrator to his dad and his granddad. And we are reminded of just how difficult it is to hold on to what we love, and how it is stories that keep our loved ones alive. Just ask Wrendon or his boy.

Steven Barthelme's story epitomizes the unreliable narrator. Probably this shouldn't be a separate category at all. The reliability of every first-person narrator is in question, since he or she has a stake in the outcome of the story, and the narrator must earn our trust—or not.

THE NEW SOUTH:
WRITING THE *NEWSWEEK* SHORT STORY

The place was full of hicks. They were eating tires, all-terrain, it's a local delicacy. It tastes like fried chicken. They were short, the ones that weren't larger than life. Okay, well, so the guy didn't say, "Knee-caps to a gee-raffe," exactly. He said, "short," that the old guy was short, but that wouldn't have been very *colorful* and everybody knows there are a lot of colorful folks down South. So when I wrote the piece, I kinda said he said something he didn't say, exactly. But gee-raffe is what he meant. Somebody did say that once, it's not like I made it up; I had an English teacher once who said that, Southern guy. There is no such thing as objectivity, I mean we all agree on that, right? He looked like a guy who was thinking, *Knee-caps.*

The stuff about the steroid poodle and the pit bull? No, that's just the way it happened. Pit bull didn't know what hit him. Little furry fella. Damnedest thing I ever saw. And that short old guy just smiled and spit tobacco juice into his Dixie cup and collected his money, got his poodle, and drove away in that Cadillac. There wasn't anyone there named "Velvet Skinned Annie," though—I stole that from an Elmore Leonard book I was reading. Damn good book, a Western. They made a movie out of it, with Paul Newman, good movie. Poodle had some abs, I tell you.

Well, and it was a pretty big poodle, like the size of a python. Well, it could've been a python. I couldn't see too well, I was in the bar, watching on closed-circuit TV, and on the screen all you could see were all those good ole boys in plaid shirts crowded around, hollering and waving bills in the air. This was right after the Rattlesnake Roundup. Tastes just like fried chicken.

Come to think of it, there was no poodle in the Cadillac, when the old guy left. He was sort of a young old guy. Left town with Velvet Skinned Annie hanging all over him and the "deppity sherff" right on his tail. Come to think of it, it was a Lexus, or a Cherokee, one of those. I've never actually been to that bar, but my brother told me about it. I'd've had to leave the apartment to go to that bar. Wait a minute, I think the magazine's calling.

It wasn't really a deputy sheriff, it was an ATF agent. Actually . . . never mind. Maybe the python was in the trunk. This is where the story gets a little hazy; I had to fill in some blanks. I did interview the PR guy from the state gaming commission and he does have a slot machine on his desk, one of those like you can buy at Service Merchandise. My brother told me.

I interviewed the guy by telephone. He did say the thing about giving a "rat's ass," that's verbatim—"Son, I don't give a redneck rat's ass whether some snake tore the peewaddle out of some moongoose." He didn't say, "Son," I polished a little. I hadn't told him it was a mongoose, I had said "mongrel," but nobody pays attention nowadays. "Peewaddle" is a word my daughter got at that Catholic school, isn't it great?

If I had a brother, I'd name him Mozart. Mozart P. Concerto, that's my real last name, Concerto. We're Italian. It wasn't a mongoose—or a "moongoose!" Goddamn, these people are colorful—it was more of a mouse-type creature. The magazine sent me to check on the pandas, how they were doing, one of them's been sick, it was some kind of Red Chinese thing, and while I was waiting for the curator I wandered into the reptile house, and a bunch of the staff—they were Pakistanis mostly, sounded like the BBC in there—were hanging around while they fed some of the snakes.

They *were* wearing plaid shirts, though. Except one had on this gorgeous topcoat. It was a big mother, Bull Snake or something. I was on deadline, and under a wee bit of pressure; the goddamn magazine hadn't used anything of mine in eleven years. I started thinking, What if I maybe just *ooonch* this a little. I have never, ever, done anything like this before, understand. Maybe this little ole mouse is a dog, some kind of colorful, Southern dog . . . You're under a certain pressure to come up with startling or fresh ideas, you know, a vision thing. May sound simple, but it isn't. Trick is to make sure they look exactly like the old ideas.

Anyway, the Pakistani, the guy with the topcoat, comes over, this really elegant guy, he sounds like Alec Guinness in *Lawrence of Arabia*, and he says, "How are you?" and "Why are you here?" and I say, "I'm a writer," and damned if he isn't a writer, too. He's from South Pakistan. Published fourteen novels. He says, "You are not writing now," and I'm getting depressed, and I say, "Why bother?" He smoothes his big gray topcoat, gazes out over the desert, shrugs, and says, "Because life is borink." At the end, the warden comes in and . . . Oh, skip it. Just ask my brother. That's exactly how it happened, only twenty years ago and the Pakistani was my English teacher and I ran into him in the hall in Parchman Hall.

And we all squeezed into his pickup truck hollerin' and cussin' and wavin' our drumsticks and our sweet cool cans of Dixie beer, shootin' our guns and corruptin' public officials and spittin', just acres of spittin'. That'll work.

Yes, your stories can be funny. Here our author explores a topic we're all too familiar with these days: journalists fabricating their stories. One *USA Today* reporter used a snapshot he took of a Cuban hotel worker to authenticate a story he made up about a woman who died fleeing Cuba by boat. The woman in the photo neither fled by boat nor died. A *New York Times* reporter made up conversations with wounded veterans that never happened. And so it goes, proving, perhaps, what we already suspect: it's all fiction.

SECOND PERSON: The pronoun *You*. In this case *You* is a character in the story, not the reader addressed by the narrator. There are two forms:

- **The reader as character:** The reader is asked to imagine herself a character in the story. This technique can draw the reader into the story if you do it right or put her off if you don't.

- **The I-substitute:** Here the second person is a not very subtle disguise for first person. Perhaps the narrator needs to distance himself from himself and from the reader, moving his ego offstage, perhaps because the material is too difficult to confront, and is asking us to imagine what it might be like to be in his situation.

Steve Almond's story is an example of the reader as character.

STOP

Or maybe you're here, Sturbridge, Mass., off the Pike, punching a register, Roy Rogers, a girl in a brown smock. America comes at you on buses, in caps and shorts, fuming. What the hell, you're killing each other, anyway. This kind of loneliness. What are words? You've got chores, duties, an inanimate world that needs you. Sometimes, late afternoon, you scrape the grill and figure: this could be love, this clean violence, the meaty shavings and steel beneath. There are other ideas out there, in magazines and movies. But you see your life, that which persists, the dumpster out back, the counter dulled by your hands, relish troughs to fill. Some days the clouds are so thick they seem weighted. You are kind and not especially pretty. You do your job. You are polite. At great expense, you smile. Your best friend died just down the road, in an accident at night. You laid a pink bear before the marker and you persisted, you persist.

———————————

The loneliness in "Stop" is palpable. I felt numbed by the dreadful daily routine and the assault of strangers. I was reminded of Thoreau's observation that most of us "lead lives of quiet desperation." I knew this very restaurant off the Pike—it's no longer there—so close to Old Sturbridge Village, a living history museum where volunteers reenact life as it was in 1830s New England, at the time Thoreau was

> What continues to interest me the most about the short-short form is that it so often serves as a vehicle for the exploration of the lyrical possibilities of prose.
>
> —*Stuart Dybek*

writing his journals and teaching school. Our author achieved the expression of powerful emotions through a set of objects, details that evoked the sadness, the hopelessness: those meaty shavings on the steel grill, the relish troughs, the smudged counter, that forlorn pink bear. And yet, our heroine persists.

———

In Nathan Leslie's short-short story, *You* is a substitute for *I*.

THE OTHER PERSON

You write the story in the second person. It's your go-to point of view now. You like its edge, its resonance of irony even if your story lacks said irony (it adds irony). You makes anything possible. You is the new me.

By writing the story in the second person you can avoid concerning yourself with psychological dimensions; you can avoid overthinking. You makes every sentence glow, you think. It makes the reader the story. It's direct engagement. It's intense. Immediacy.

It's like a camera down the gullet. It's like being inside someone. It's like sex, without the emotional messiness.

Your story is about an anonymous man (or woman perhaps—though most yous are men) who walks through the urban blight, looking for a child named Cass. You had just heard the Mamas & the Papas on the Classics station, and hadn't really thought about Mama Cass for years. Cass? Why not Cass? You like the allusion.

Hipsters should know.

Fiction should educate. The urban blight is somewhat inspired by the city in which you live, though a far more post-apocalyptic version thereof. Instead of Starbucks and little pastry shops and Thai restaurants with orchids on every table you write about the desiccated skeletons of once-productive textile factories, crack vials, and prostitutes with scabs on their faces. You've never seen desiccated textile factories, crack vials, or prostitutes (scabs or scab-free), but you use your imagination. If you don't know, *you* will. Zombies, there's always zombies. Second-person zombies.

You wonder, Why the post-apocalyptic mélange? In a more or less peaceful age you notice more horrific violence, more dripping pipes and sunless urban canyons. Yet from whence does this come? You know the recession hasn't helped, but aren't zombies an overreaction? Are you really living in an urban wasteland? There's a Whole Foods on every other corner. Shit's nice.

Once, just once, you'd like to meet a reader. This would help clarify your purpose. And not a reader-who-is-also-a-writer hawking his latest "fabulist" novella at AWP ("It's like *1Q84*, only shorter, and less, you know, Japanese")—a real reader. One who just reads, doesn't write. Even more ideal would be catching a reader in the middle of reading one of your stories, midstream, so to speak. You'd love to ask the reader if he/she felt as if she/he was the protagonist. You'd love to know if she/he was walking through the rat-infested heroin streets whilst searching for Cass. And if he/she felt as if he/she could place himself/herself in the story, did you feel invested in it? Did you feel the intensity of the *you*? Did you meld with the story? Did the fourth wall come crumbling down?

You keep your eyes peeled. You've published in several small magazines, but you never see people out and about in society reading the *Orange Toad Belly Review* (circulation 250). Even if you positioned yourself on the campus of Southwestern Central Missouri State Community College (South Bend Campus), you doubt you would see people walking around reading the *Orange Toad Belly*

Review. They're in a box somewhere in some professor's office. Behind some other boxes of other shit he's been meaning to get to.

But then. You're on the Metro people-watching through the reflection in the window. Through the reflection you see a young woman scrolling on her iPad. She clicks on several literary pages, then—amazingly—clicks on the *Orange Toad Belly Review.* You watch her scanning the page, then she clicks on your story.

Ten seconds is a long time, you think. For ten seconds your story, "Gristle and Bone," lingers on her screen. It does more than linger. It pulses. It, like, *throbs* on her screen. She's reading it. You aren't breathing. You are watching her read. A real person, reading.

You hold your breath. For the first in time your life you feel as if you are really and truly an author. You feel as if you have a voice and someone wants to hear it. You feel as if you could be the author you've always wanted to be—an amalgam of Pynchon and Vonnegut with a dash of Rushdie and Márquez and a dusting of Barthelme. You feel important.

She utters a quick little snort. Then she clicks away. She clicks to Facebook.

"Wait, wait, wait," you say, startled by the intensity of your reaction. You turn your head.

"Huh?" the reader says.

"Just . . . why did you click away from that last piece?"

"Are you, like, spying on what I'm looking at?"

"No."

"Yes, you are. It's, you know, really none of your business."

"Ordinarily, I'd agree, but I wrote that."

"You wrote that?"

"Yeah. So I was wondering. Why did you click away?"

She says she doesn't know. It just didn't appeal to her. It was too negative. Too caustic. It didn't have the human dimension she's looking for in a story. It was missing something. Plus the whole "you" thing is weird, isn't it? It feels forced. Am I supposed to be that person, or something? I'm not. I'm me. She snorted. *Snorted.*

"I see," you say.

"Sorry," she says, and lowers her head back to her iPad. "Gotta be honest."

You wander down the streets of your pleasant urban reality. The craft shops seemed to have tripled in the past three years. You pass three grocery stores in three blocks. Now there's a tea shop. More bagel shoppes than you can count. Aren't those little art galleries precious? You can't help but peek inside one or two crystal shops. Or is that you? You're not sure anymore.

You plop down on your "reclaimed" vintage sofa you bought for $1,687 at Dukents, the new furniture boutique down on Twelfth Street. It probably cost $100 to make back in 1979, or whatever. Now it's "vintage." Perhaps you should invest in furniture, you think. You close your eyes and breathe and listen to your breathing. It's good to be alive, you think. One day you will write something good. You know you will. You'll keep trying. Your ten seconds will be elongated. You will become loved. We all should, shouldn't we? Isn't that what this is all about?

––––––––––

What delightful and hilarious insights into second-person narratives. All the reasons to use it right there in the second paragraph. The I-substitute You distances the narrator from himself—he's an anonymous man and certainly nothing at all like the narrator or author. What can go wrong with the *reader as character* form: "Am I supposed to be that person, or something? I'm not." Here's everything you need to know about second-person point of view—shown and not told.

> You can't use up creativity. The more you use, the more you have.
>
> —*Maya Angelou*

THIRD PERSON: The pronouns *He* or *She*. Several forms here.

Objective: Also called the dramatic, camera lens, or fly-on-the-wall technique. What you see is all you get. There is no access to thoughts or feelings of any character. Shirley Jackson's "The Lottery" is often cited as an example of dramatic point of view. Think of watching a play. Or a trial. Here's a found short-short story taken from the transcript of the murder trial of Lizzie Borden that appeared in a Fall River daily newspaper. Imagine yourself in the jury box or the gallery.

THE BREAKING OF AN EGG

Mr. Jennings: Now let me go a little further and see if I can refresh your recollection. Don't you remember that Mrs. Holmes was there that afternoon and you had some conversation about an egg?
Hannah Reagan: About what?

Q. About an egg.

A. I remember about the egg, but I couldn't tell you whether it was that afternoon or not, sir.

Q. What was it about the egg?

A. The breaking of an egg.

Q. Well, what was said or done?

A. We were talking in the afternoon, me and Lizzie Borden, and I says, "I can tell you one thing you can't do," and she says, "Tell me what it is, Mrs. Reagan." I says, "Break an egg, Miss Borden," and she says, "Break an egg?" I says, "Yes." "Well," she says, "I can break an egg." I says, "Not the way I would tell you to break it." She says, "Well, what way is it, Mrs. Reagan?" So I told her that she couldn't break it the way I wanted her to break it, and I said I would bet her a dollar that she couldn't, and she said she would bet me a quarter, and in the afternoon someone fetched Lizzie an egg, and Miss Emma Borden was sitting down beside her, and I told Miss Emma Borden to get a little ways away, "Because," I said, "if she will break the egg the wrong way it will destroy your dress," and she did get the egg, and she got it in her hands, and she couldn't break it, and she says, "There," she says, "that is the first thing that I undertook to do that I never could."

Limited: Also called third-person attached. Here we get the thoughts and feelings of the central character and no one else, but we're not confined to the character's mind. Here's Steven Barthelme once again.

SALE

Quinn sold the car one Friday morning in the parking lot of his new apartment complex. The buyer trembled as the two of them walked around the car. A skinny, very fair man in a pink oxford shirt, deathly pale in the morning sunlight. When he reached out and ran his finger along a deep crease in the front fender, Quinn nodded. "That dent tells a story," he said, and laughed. The guy crouched and stared hard down the length of the car, looking for waves in the body panels. Something he read in a magazine article, Quinn thought. He can't see a thing. Jesus, somebody should tell him not to wear pink shirts. Looks like the inside of a watermelon. Name is probably Allen or something. The man stood by the driver's door, staring inside.

"My wife's car," Quinn said. "Ex-wife. Her ex-car. She . . . she— We're divorced. She spent too much time with the neighbor down the street."

"Looks in good shape," the pale guy said.

Quinn nodded. "He was on television, a weatherman; on weekends. She thought he was some kind of star." Jesus, he thought. His face. Watermelon rind.

"Can we start it up?" the guy said.

"What? Sure, here." Quinn handed him the keys. "Need to goose it a couple times, get some gas on the way."

The guy started the car. "You mind if I have a friend of mine look it over?" He sat in the driver's seat with one leg hanging out the open door and leaned forward, listening to the engine. "That ticking normal?"

Quinn shrugged. "I know from ticking, right? How about nine hundred? Two bills for ticking. You know that dent I showed you?" Quinn said. "They were parked in front of the house, one night. I was inside, watching *Masterpiece Theatre*, and I heard brakes and then this shriek, like somebody pulling a rack out of a gigantic oven. I ran outside and there was my wife and the weatherman, and some kid with one of those stupid trucks, the ones way up in the air with the airplane tires?

"My wife was buttoning her shirt. The weatherman, he's giving the kid a hundred bucks, a hundred-dollar bill. He's doing my wife right on the street in front of my house, and he carries around hundred-dollar bills." Quinn looked around the perfect, empty parking lot. "So I moved here." The apartments were red brick, almost orange. A low chain-link fence ran along the edge of the parking lot.

"I'm sorry," the guy said.

"She didn't want to be ordinary, I guess. And he was on TV." Quinn drew himself full height and threw his arm out, drawing in the air with a finger. "You know, pointing to those swirly lines with the pimples." He screwed up his face in a lurid smile. "It's a cold front, here . . . so get out the fuzzy wuzzies tonight—" His hand hung in the air, pointing to an imaginary map. "Stars," he said, and shook his head. "I still watch him, every weekend."

The pale guy looked at the car.

"Why don't you just take it?" Quinn said. "Just get it out of here." The car was a big green Chrysler, nine years old. It looked stupid in the parking lot, in the evenings, when all the Hondas and Toyotas and the GM copies of them and a few Jaguars and Corvettes and one black Porsche came home. "Just take it. Have you got ten bucks?"

"I'm really sorry."

Quinn laughed. "Hey, don't be. That's life, right? Thing that bothers me is, I wanted to call the cops. I mean that's what I thought: Call the cops; get the kid a ticket; square it with the insurance. But he was right. Give the kid a hundred dollars. Burns me up. That's what we have stars for. They always know what to do." He smiled.

In a green car, Quinn thought, he looks even stranger. Extraordinary. People'll say, Allen, where'd you get that car? Hey everybody! Look at Allen's new car.

———

Every dent, like every wound, tells a story. Our befuddled cuckold Quinn is trying to move on, but he can't quite do it. Allen thinks he's buying a used Chrysler, but he's getting something that might be more valuable—a story. Quinn ironically looks to the neighbor who stole his wife for direction. The man's a star, after all, and he knows what to do, knows which way the wind blows.

Multiple Selective Omniscience: The viewpoint shifts from one character to another, sometimes to several others. (But that's unlikely in a very short story.) The trick here is not to confuse the reader about whose consciousness we are in. This is a way to get more than one take on a situation. Bonnie Losak utilizes multiple POV in her story.

THE RIVER'S DAUGHTER

Riley learned she was pregnant just three weeks before her forty-second birthday. She wasn't married and certainly hadn't planned to start a family. There had been talk of kids earlier, sure, but that was when she was still with Devon. Now that Devon had moved out, Riley was glad they had put off having kids. Just the thought of having to share a child of hers, even an imaginary child, with Devon and his new girlfriend, made her bring up bile, even now.

After the divorce, Riley moved to a two-bedroom cottage just uphill from the Staley River. There, she taught piano to the neighborhood children and tried her hand at gardening. Riley met Emerson at the farmers' market two years later. She watched as he shook a half dozen cantaloupes close to his ear and then moved on to begin his assault on the grapefruit. He was an accountant, she learned, with two ex-wives and one grown son. It was an uneven relationship, but the passion persisted, and after two years, they were still together.

"Are you sure?" Emerson had asked that Sunday morning, rising and circling the blue Adirondack chair that occupied the south corner of Riley's deck.

Riley nodded. She was only six weeks along but already her nipples had darkened and her stomach lurched when she stood, making her feel like she had just stepped off a carousel that was spinning improbably fast.

Emerson smoothed back his graying curls and then scratched at the weekend stubble he had let settle in. Behind him, a trio of low-lying clouds merged and scattered again.

"But . . ." Emerson said.

"I know." Riley's voice was flat. "It's not foolproof."

Emerson leaned on the railing of the deck and looked out to the spot where Riley was trying to coax strawberries and watermelon to spring up from the earth. The wind shifted. "Rain's just on the other side of the river," Emerson said. "Feel that?"

Riley didn't answer. Instead, she studied the sharp edge of the deck where the irregular shadow of a potted geranium had begun to shift and fade. Then she inhaled and the scent of those damp, smooth stones that lined the riverbed filled her nostrils.

In the ensuing silence, Emerson took in Riley's short blond hair and the freckles that lingered on either side of her nose. He let his gaze drift downward. Were Riley's breasts swollen? He couldn't tell. And her belly? No. Looked the same to him.

In order to give himself time to think, if only for a moment, Emerson walked over to the beveled glass table that sidled up against the railing and pulled out a wrought-iron chair. Then, lifting his chin in Riley's direction, Emerson said, "What do you want to do?"

Riley raised a shoulder. "I don't know." She hesitated. "Have it, I guess."

"Really?" Emerson lifted one brow in that way he had.

Riley pulled in her lips.

"You sure?" Emerson asked.

"Sort of."

"How long have you known?"

"Not long."

"Do you want to think about it more?"

Riley shook her head.

"But what if something goes wrong?"

"Don't say that."

"You can't ignore it."

"They do tests. All sorts of tests."

"The tests aren't foolproof, you know."

Riley chewed the skin on the outside of her thumbnail until she tasted blood. Then she got up to spit the piece of skin out by the railing and started coughing for no reason.

"You okay?" Emerson asked.

Riley nodded.

"I'm not sure this is a good idea," he said.

"You think I should get an abortion, Em?"

Emerson shrugged.

Riley put a hand to her mouth and swallowed back a foul-tasting belch. "If you want me to get an abortion, you should at least have the nerve to come out and say it." Riley's voice was rising, quavering in that way it did when she got mad. She hated that voice. It sounded weak, whiny, even to her.

"I don't want you to get an abortion. I just . . . I just think we should at least consider it."

Riley stood up and walked down the steps of the deck toward the river. By the time she could hear the lapping of the water on the blue stones that gathered at the water's edge, the rain had started. When she got back to the deck, her socks and sneakers were wet and her hair was dripping down her back. Emerson wasn't on the deck or under the eave. Riley decided that he must have gone home (wouldn't that be just like him?) when he appeared at the storm door with a towel and a steaming cup of tea.

Six months into the pregnancy, Riley began having contractions. The doctors did what they could to stop the labor, but Allegra pushed her way out during Riley's twenty-fifth week of pregnancy. She was not much bigger than Emerson's outstretched palm. Riley knew that Allegra's chances weren't good. Her skin was an odd color of translucent red and her dark eyes seemed dull and sunken. She was placed in the neonatal ICU with a roomful of other premature babies. Riley tried not to look at the other infants. Through Riley's tired eyes, they all seemed misshapen, malformed, more birdlike than human.

At first, Riley and Emerson would position themselves on either side of Allegra's plastic incubator and just caress their baby's tiny hands and paper-thin skin. Then, when Emerson's paperwork began to pile up at the office, Riley would tend to Allegra alone, singing to her in hushed tones. Riley sang old lullabies she hadn't heard before and hymns from church services she never attended. When Riley sang, the tension that pulled at Allegra's every vein—the sheer work of staying alive, Emerson had called it—seemed to slacken, and Riley imagined she saw a flicker of light pass through Allegra's eyes.

At six days old, though, Allegra stopped breathing. A blue-gray color that Riley had already learned to associate with death, settled on Allegra's lips and the skin above her mouth even before the alarm sounded. As one nurse arrived at Allegra's incubator, another guided Riley out of the NICU.

In the waiting room, Riley sat at the edge of a vinyl-backed chair and stared at the paisley wallpaper until it resembled pink infants huddled together in one large incubator, swaying back and forth. Shivering, Riley stood up and positioned herself at a far corner of the room, where a long, rectangular window let in just a sliver of light. There, she started to sing to Allegra in that low hushed tone. She sang those songs that no one had taught her and that later, sitting at the piano in her cottage by the lake again, she wouldn't be able to remember. If only I can keep singing, thought Riley, Allegra will hear me. She will take that breath. She will finally come home.

Riley didn't remember falling asleep, or even sitting back down. It could have been ten minutes. It could have been two hours. Emerson was beside her now, his glasses off, his eyes wet. The doctor was leaning over, stroking her arm. But his words were garbled, muffled. Riley couldn't make them out. All she could hear was the river calling out to her as it rushed toward that bed of smooth, blue stones.

We get our trouble right away: an unexpected pregnancy relatively late in life and the landscape littered with broken marriages. Here the narrator stays out of the way, moving deftly between our two characters as they deal with each other and what will surely be a drastic change in their lives. We understand Emerson's concerns and admire his honesty. This is a story about something important. This is a story that takes an ax to the frozen sea within us: the startling scent of damp, smooth stones, the terrified parents at the incubator, and Allegra's heroic struggle, "the sheer work of staying alive." So much temptation to get lost in sentimentality, but not a false step is taken.

——

Omniscient: The narrator as all-knowing god. The almighty voice of the epic. Can know anything about any character, can be in any place at any time, past, present, future. Is this even appropriate in a very short story? A problem with the omniscient narrator is focus, as you might have guessed. He can tell all, but he shouldn't. Here Jason Marc Harris writes a very short story about an amazing flying boy that might remind you of the Icarus and Daedalus myth.

FALLEN

Before the boy fell, tourists milled about the edge of Crater Lake, midnight blue a thousand feet below. Families posed by the low wall, dividing sidewalk from gaping cliffs of the caldera, Nature's exhaust port of buried molten fury.

Sitting on a picnic table, a freckled fat kid wearing overalls sucked on a lollipop while Pops swilled beer. Pops occasionally glanced back at his pickup truck where his wife had nodded off in the front passenger's seat.

Two teenage sisters and two teenage brothers laughed, rocking on that wall beneath yellow sign warning about death-by-cliffs. Bald, bearded Papà with glasses muttered, "Non sio muovono," and rechecked the settings on his camera, propped up on a thick tripod, an alien insect poised to twitch across the road into the woods.

A small Mexican boy tapped the top of the wall with his stick while his smaller brother and sister sang behind him on the other side of the wall, along the band of dry even ground patched with dirty snow.

Past this strip, the cliff arced downwards, flecked by stubborn dwarfish firs and dotted by boulders poking out from snowdrifts that sloped more and more steeply to a vanishing point where cliff met the water's surface.

Smiling with folded arms and raised eyebrows beneath a baseball cap, corners of his lips disappearing beneath thick moustache, Padré watched his kids' progress along the wall.

His wife pushed the baby carriage, holding a fourth child who shook a small pink rattle, a rhythm of fits and starts punctuated by her gurgling cry. "Silencio, silencio," the mother whispered, stroking curly braids.

Gasping from the brief hike from the lower parking lot to the overlook, an aging motorcyclist, Mr. Muir, glanced at the fathers with their families as he smoked his cigar and stared out at Wizard Island, the lone isle poking up a few hundred feet above the azure waters. Cold as hell down there. He'd tested the water more than once. In younger days, he'd hiked the trail down to the boat launch in the last thirty years he'd been visiting Crater Lake National Park.

Mr. Muir's wheezing disturbed a tall woman with green hair and a jacket far too dark and warm for the June sun. As she stared out at the tranquil blue, voices in her head kept urging her the way they usually did when she neared some precipice. "Jump, Ally! Just go ahead and jump!" Would she jump today? If she left this miserable world, her last thoughts might be: "How wonderful"—as pure beauty immersed her.

The hot stench of Mr. Muir's sweat and cigar seeped into her nostrils. A couple of voices politely suggested that she push the "red-faced capitalist pig" over the edge, but he was as solidly planted as the stony benches sunk on the paved path bordering the caldera.

A long-haired thin man with both ears pierced with what looked like wine-bottle corks scowled at Mr. Muir as he passed by. The hippie's girlfriend, wearing a "Grow Organic" purple shirt, coughed and glared at Mr. Muir too, whose eyes smoldered with amusement as he exhaled in their direction.

"Schau mich an! Vater!" A blond-haired, blue-eyed child had climbed to the top of a mound of snow about level with the top of the wall.

"Gunter, sehr gut! Very good!" Vater praised him while squinting at the camera. His wife with her long hair wrapped up in a ponytail smiled and nodded at the boy, who stared with a grin so wide and fixed it seemed paralyzed by delight.

Ally watched the child's smile. The voices were silenced. What did this child have to tell her today as it danced in front of its vater and mütter? This shining elf upon the mound of snow?

The boy's right foot slipped forward.

His left foot slid back, catching the lip of the wall and propelling the child backwards over the wall in a lopsided somersault.

He screamed as he fell. A jowl of fat pushed up from underneath his chin, giving him the uncanny face of a startled yowling marshmallow.

Mesmerized by this procession of mortality, Ally envied and feared the terror and release the child must feel, hurtling headlong into the abyss of blue.

Then she vomited.

"Gunter! Gunter!"

His father had dropped the camera, which landed with a loud crack on the pavement.

He clutched the air above where his son was rolling, spinning into a slide that carried him with a shriek out of sight beyond the bony snags of trees that somehow perpetually clamped into the sheer angle of the cliff. His wife had her arms around her husband as she sobbed and stared down the slope.

"Shit!" Mr. Muir said, hobbling over to the cliff next to the screaming German.

The Mexican father turned around, barked something to the brothers and sister on the wrong side of the wall. His children came scampering close like a group of young quail.

The Italians all got up, jabbering in a frenzy of whispers, and hovered a dozen feet away from where the bereaved German father continued to call down the rocky side of the caldera.

"Gunter! Gunter!"

Mr. Muir's fingers burned, so he dropped his cigar and stomped it out.

Italians, Germans, Mexicans, and various Americans swarmed the low wall.

Hippie guy had already run across the street to the visitor center and shouted the tale of woe to the ranger on duty. The search would be on, and another body would be culled from the icy waters below.

"My God, my G-God," the shuddering hippie girlfriend repeated in a breathy chant.

Ally wandered in a nauseous daze, mouth soured and burning, along the low wall.

"See?" the voices whispered. "A religious experience. Blue darkness. Sacred death."

But she had stopped listening to them.

The Clark's nutcracker clicked and knocked in the distance while billowing cumulus clouds began their gradual march across the sky.

All the tourists stared down at the waters, seeing nothing but what they had seen before.

———————

Know It All

Follow these directions for writing a very short story in the third-person omniscient point of view.

1. Get your two characters together. Where are they? Give us the details of the place. Use your five senses. They're talking. What else are they doing? Give these two people names.

2. Character A wants something from Character B. What is it? Love? Money? Forgiveness? Understanding? Something more sinister? Why does A want it? Character B is unwilling to cooperate. Why?

3. Put us in A's consciousness. Let us know what he or she is thinking and feeling as they speak and do whatever it is they're doing.

4. Do the same for B.

5. The narrator interrupts for a moment to let us know that one of the two characters is keeping a secret and the other is lying. What is the secret? What is the lie? How does this knowledge affect our reading of the story?

6. Get us back to the conversation. Let A struggle to get what he or she wants. Resolve the story. She gets it or doesn't.

The Qualities of a Good Short-Short Story

Part of the fun of writing them is the sense of slipping between the seams. Within the constraint of their small boundaries the writer discovers great freedom. In fact, their very limitations of scale also demand unconventional strategies.

—STUART DYBEK

THIS MIGHT be a good time to think about what constitutes a very good very short story. Let's read one, a very brilliant one, and it's by Natalia Rachel Singer.

HONEYCOMB

Mrs. Stick stood breathless in her kitchen stirring rutabagas and pigs' knuckles into a heavy stew. She was expecting Mr. Mann, who had the produce stand in the next district where every day a gang of quarreling farmers came to weigh their squash and sugar beets on the dusty scale in his pickup. Mr. Mann was lean and oily, with black bristles of hair that could paint her belly honey yellow in flat wide strokes. She wanted him to want her

but she knew he liked his women meatier, with thick toenails that could click against his like castanets. Mrs. Stick
hummed the score from *Oklahoma!* and waited, feeling
desire part her like a comb.

When the stew was ready, she skimmed off the scum
and tossed it onto her mulch pile beneath the only living
elm tree in the country, two paces from her baby's grave.
She thought of those eyelids less yielding than a doll's, that
unbearable silence, felt the old hollow ache as wind rushed
up her ash-colored skirt. When she opened her eyes again
there he was, real as grain, riding across the valley, the dust
fluttering behind like a cloud of worker bees. His truck
galumphed; there were mounds of squash pounding up and
down just for her.

"How much does a baby weigh?" he'd ask her when she
exclaimed how big they were, how perfectly whole. After
their meal they'd walk to the river while the last of the sun
spit honey, their clasped fingers shortening the stretch of
empty fields.

———————

Notice how attention to language and sound here is as exact as
we've come to expect it from poetry. Perhaps the compression of
the very short, the micro, form demands it.

- **Title:** *Honeycomb* is a compound word in which the whole
  is more than the sum of its parts. *Honey*—that sweet
  viscous fluid that is the nectar of flowers and that figura-
  tively means sweetness and is also a term of endearment.

Comb—a strip of metal, wood, bone with teeth used for disentangling, cleaning, arranging the hair and like purposes. And we see uses of both nouns in the story, the comb that parts her desire, the honey spit by the sun. *Honey* is also used as an adjective describing a delicious shade of yellow. And the whole: the *honeycomb*—a structure of wax containing two series of hexagonal cells separated by thin partitions, formed by bees for the reception of honey and eggs. And that might suggest her reception of a sweet viscous fluid in the matrix of her womb, which might, in turn, suggest plot and motivation.

- **Names:** *Mrs. Stick* and *Mr. Mann.* She a rod or piece of wood, suggesting her slim, twiggy size, perhaps. The metaphorical meaning of a stick as a wooden person is in play, and we'll see if it applies. *Mann* is the German for *man,* and this might suggest the anonymity of an average Joe.

- **Sound devices:** *onomatopoeia:* that galumphing truck; *assonance:* "mounds of squash pounding"; "dust fluttering" "thick, click"; *alliteration:* "shortening the stretch" *consonance:* "she skimmed off the scum."

- **Figurative language:** the *metaphor* of Mr. Mann as a paintbrush and of desire "that parts her like a comb"; the disturbing, if hilarious, *simile* of toenails as castanets; the dust like a cloud of worker bees; Mr. Mann real as grain; the *personification* of the spitting sun.

- **The precise word:** The grave is two *paces* from the tree, not steps or feet or yards. Two paces meaning the distance covered in two steps, indicating approximate distance and suggesting an antiquated unit of measure that seems appropriate with the rather rudimentary agriculture in the next district. Mr. Mann is *riding*, not driving, across the valley, a word that conjures the American cowboy and transforms the ordinary Mann to mythic hero. They clasp *fingers*, not hands, the five terminal members of the hand, but not the entire hand, suggesting, perhaps, caution or skittishness.

And it's not only attention to language but attention to vivid and significant detail. This is a story of desire and nourishment. Mrs. Stick wants Mr. Mann, and she's going to get to his heart through his stomach. Cooking is an act of love. Note the food—simple, basic, and unmodified: rutabagas, pigs' knuckles; squash, sugar beets. A couple of root vegetables and squash suggesting a late-season harvest, and the knuckles suggesting flavor more than nutrition. Other details—he is lean and oily; the scale is dusty; the doll's and baby's eyelids are haunting and unyielding; the ash-colored skirt; those clasped fingers; the empty fields. All the details helping to set the tone.

And there is a plot though it is not all on the page. Let me reiterate what a traditional plot is. Aristotle told us that plots have beginnings, middles, and ends and that complex plots, the best plots, proceed through a series of reversals and recognitions. A reversal is a change in a situation to its opposite. A recognition is a change from ignorance to knowledge. Oedipus now understands the terrible truth that he had struggled to learn. Remember John Gardner's definition: The basic plot of all stories is: you have a central character who wants something and goes after it despite opposition, and, as a result of a struggle, comes to a win or a loss.

Mrs. Stick, as I've said, wants Mr. Mann to love her, and we know why. At the center of the story is a catastrophic loss—the death of a child. And here we might pause to consider a missing character. Mr. Stick—she is a Missus, not a Miss. Did the death of the child mean the death of the marriage? We don't know. But whatever happened, Mr. Stick is not around to fulfill his husbandly duties. And, apparently, the gang of quarreling farmers won't do. Mr. Mann, who enjoys more zaftig ladies, is the owner of a scale and a truck. She cooks and he comes. First paragraph, Act I, the set-up; second paragraph, Act II, the buildup. And then Act III of our drama in the final paragraph—the payoff. And here the story leaps ahead into the near future through Mrs. Stick's point of view. In fact, the shift begins in the last sentence of paragraph two—she imagines all the squash is for her. The final act, then, is one of hope, that this is what will happen—she will get what she wants. When she remarks about the quality of the squash—how big and whole— he asks a question of quantity: How much do babies weigh? Which leads me to another notion about this story specifically and art generally.

Coleridge said there can be no great art without a certain strangeness. By strangeness he didn't mean bizarre or zany, but rather having the quality of being unfamiliar, uncommon, unusual, extraordinary, something that doesn't quite belong. And this story has a certain strangeness, I think, a mix of the domestic and ordinary with the odd and perplexing. Our lives are deadened by routine. Art makes the familiar strange again. "There is no excellent beauty that hath not some strangeness in the proportion," wrote Francis Bacon.

- Mrs. Stick doesn't stand; she stands "breathless."
- The "next district" suggests some archaic political system.

- The lean and oily Mr. Mann, like a deep-fried potato.
- Those horny toenails.
- She's humming show tunes, which seems incongruous.
- There's only one elm tree in the whole country! (Dutch elm disease notwithstanding.)
- The baby's grave is not in a cemetery, but by the tree and the mulch pile.

With those thoughts about "Honeycomb," let's try writing a very short story.

A Man and a Woman

A man and a woman in a room. This is Providence, Rhode Island. He wears gold cuff links in the shape of arrows on his white shirt-sleeves and a matching tie bar over his silk tie. She seems preoc-cupied. She holds a glass in her hand. Write their story in three hundred words. Use the word *salvation* and the word *light*. Make one of the pair your central character and construct the story from his or her point of view. Set your timer for thirty minutes. You're just trying to get black on white right now, just aiming for a first draft. Remember *figurative language, the precise word, the vivid and significant details, the characters, the setting, the title, the certain strangeness*. Think about secrets. Both of your characters have a secret. What are they? The secrets will inform the scene whether they are revealed or not. Think about lies. Of omission or commission. Lies that deceive, that cover up, that protect. Think about the year, the time of day, the season. Use all of your senses.

When you're done, put it away. Take it out later in the week and begin the next draft, when you will take an even closer look at the precise words, the metaphors, the sound devices, and so on.

With our aesthetic criteria in mind, let's take a look at another riveting short-short story, this one by Lee Martin.

WRONG NUMBER

The phone rings, and it's a woman with her backbone up because she knows—don't think she doesn't—that I was with her man last night.

Better keep myself distant from him, she warns, better stay away from her Buzzard, or else she'll be forced to put the hurt on me, swear to God, just see if she won't.

"I'm not playing, missy," she says. "I know where you live."

I put her on speakerphone, and my husband, Stephen, and I listen to her go on and on. Buzzard's her man and has been for twenty-five years. Her silver anniversary man, her all-day-long and nighttime man. "You go after your own," she says to me. "Piece of trash that you are. You go see what you can get."

Stephen rolls my wheelchair out onto the deck. He leaves the sliding door open so we can still hear the woman's angry voice. Since the car accident, I've lived in this chair, all sensation gone from my breastbone down. I've rolled through life, I like to say, and I've been blessed with the love of a good man who tells me he never wishes for more than what we have: a tender life, a kind life, one full of mercy and small blessings.

"Home-wrecker," he says to me with a smile.

"Oh, baby," I say with a wink. "You don't know the half of it."

The sun warms my face. A hummingbird hovers at the feeder. A car goes by, and the bass from the CD player thumps. I can feel it in my throat. I give thanks for the vibration. I close my eyes and hold on to it.

Then Stephen is kneeling beside me. He has my face in his hands, and he's kissing me, kissing me hard, a kiss I can only call hungry. A kiss that I fear tells me everything he's never been able to say about want and regret and the woman he wishes I could be. For a moment I wish it, too. I wish I were the sort who might sneak out some night with a man named Buzzard, his wife be damned. Nothing on my mind but the good times, and the baby-hey-baby, and the look in my man's eyes, as full of want and gimme as any one soul can muster.

But I'm not. I'm who I am. Only now, for the briefest of moments, the woman on the phone still talking—"Slut," she says. "I bet you've fucked so many guys you can't close your legs anymore."—I'm who we all want me to be. The woman on the phone, Stephen, me. I'm a woman with options. A woman Stephen presses to him now. A woman he fears he might lose. A woman another man might want so much he'd do something crazy, something he'd never be able to take back.

The thumping bass fades as the car drives away. I don't want to open my eyes. I don't want to look at Stephen. I don't want to think of the next things we'll say, or more than likely what we won't. I just want to sit here until the woman on the phone stops talking. I want to think about that moment when she realizes I'm gone, when she's said everything she's called to say and knows it's not enough— will never be enough. I want her to feel like there's an itch she can't quite scratch. Maybe it'll be a tingle, just the slightest stir. If only she could reach it. I want her to ache like that.

———————

A story's title is always significant. It breaks the silence and welcomes the reader into the world of the narrative. It may announce the subject matter, introduce the central character, set the tone, establish the setting or the atmosphere. The title might be an arresting central image or an allusion or a symbol. You may use your title as the first line of your story as some writers do with their poems. Doing so might give the story a sense of energy and urgency. In our story, Lee provides us with the narrative premise—a wrong number.

> A good title should be like a good metaphor; it should intrigue without being too baffling or too obvious.
>
> —*Walker Percy*

And we'll soon learn that the telephone number is not the only thing wrong in the story. The call ignites the plot, but is of no real significance itself. We might call it a MacGuffin. Our narrator never engages with the errant caller and never corrects the error.

Here we have the story of two marriages, one with enduring

trouble, the other with acute distress, of two unnamed women, and of two men, Stephen, who is present, attentive, and faithful; and Buzzard, who is absent, inattentive, and apparently unfaithful. Buzzard's name tells us all we need to know about him. He is a raptor, from the Latin for one that plunders, kidnaps, and ravishes, a bird of prey. The American buzzard is actually a turkey vulture, a scavenger, graceful in flight, but ungainly on the ground.* Stephen's familiar name suggests his ordinariness, Everyman, or Anyman, if you will.

For the admirable use of the precise word, we need look no further than the first line: to the woman with "her backbone up." The usual idiom for one extremely insulted or irritated is "hackles up." Feathers or hair, not bones. Why *backbone*? Because it resonates shortly with our narrator's *breastbone*. And we note the precise and ironic use of the verb *roll* in the clause "I've rolled through life," a usage that more readily suggests ease than effort. Our narrator doesn't *sit* in that chair; she *lives* in it.

Our author uses one of the oldest literary devices, anaphora, a sound device favored by writers of the Old Testament. It is the deliberate repetition of the opening words of successive sentences or clauses, resulting in a kind of hypnotic refrain. In fact, in the second half of our story, we get four kisses, followed by (the requisite) three wishes, followed by five "woman," followed by a litany of *want*, a word used eleven times, and in eight of the last nine sentences.

We also get our figurative language in the personified hungry kiss and in the colorful language of our two women: one threatening to "put the hurt" on the other; one described as a "piece of trash," who later grows full of "want and gimme." And

---

* To be certain, I asked Lee if by *buzzard* he meant the bird we sometimes call a turkey vulture. It was indeed.

we have the certain strangeness in that raised backbone and in our narrator's visceral response to noise, that bass sound that she feels in her throat and her closing her eyes to keep it there. Gorgeous writing.

We open with an intrusion. The telephone rings—always a moment of suspense* for the character, the reader, and the writer, who are all asking the same questions: Who's calling? And what do they want? In our case, an irate wife is calling to strike fear into the heart of the jezebel who's been cheating with her husband. Her accusation is proven false by a pair of surprises, the first amusing, the second sobering. Our narrator shares the call with her husband, and she is paralyzed from the chest down.

Which brings us to the story of a solid but circumscribed marriage, as our narrator considers her loss, her hunger, her fears, and her surprising envy of the actual jezebel, a "woman with options." At the core of the story this remarkable and achingly beautiful sentence about a prayerful and articulate kiss "that I fear tells me everything he's never been able to say about want and regret and the woman he wishes I could be." You need to catch your breath after that. "Wrong Number" is a story about what we want and what we need, who we might be and who we are. It's a story as tender, kind, and merciful as an enduring marriage. And in the end we are left with questions and with a mystery: Misdial or misdeed? Is Buzzard protecting his inamorata with a wrong number? Will the caller's grit and desire save her marriage to the philandering Buzzard? Who is this other woman anyway? Is hers a third marriage in the mix? Every story is many stories.

---

* As are every knock on the door, tap on the shoulder, muffled sound in the dark, every lump on your body that wasn't there yesterday.

The Right Number

Let's write the second act of "Wrong Number" in, say, five hundred words. While his wife is berating some woman across town, Buzzard calls his girlfriend's actual number on his cell. Sweetie, let's call her for now, is alarmed and cautious. He knows better than to call here and at this time. He tells her that his wife knows everything. We need to call it off. Sweetie says, No, we're not calling it off. She says *this* is what's going to happen. That's not possible, he says. He wants out, but she won't open the escape hatch. Write the contentious phone call. Surprise us. Don't be afraid to make us laugh or to make us gasp. They both seem like desperate people, don't they? Desperate people take desperate measures.

Words of Wisdom

Remember the words of wisdom your parents shared with you so often you thought you'd scream if you heard them one more time. "Neither a borrower or a lender be"; "You judge a man by the company he keeps"; "If all your friends jumped off a bridge, would you?"; "Children should be seen and not heard"; "Keep your eye on the ball"; "Do as I say, not as I do." Make a list of the ones you remember. Do you still live by those rules? What do you think of them now? Do you use them? Spend some time recalling and writing about these aphorisms. Then pick the one that brought back the strongest feelings or the one that seems particularly fertile. Make it the title of your new 250-word story. And just to help you along, here are some words you need to use: *fasten, rain, irregular, linoleum, grace, left*. Only 244 words to go. Begin.

Talking in Bed

Anthony Trollope suggested a writing exercise in which characters in a conversation don't listen to each other, which is often the case in real life. Philip Larkin's poem "Talking in Bed" addresses the difficulty of conversation between intimates. It should be easy, but it becomes hard to find "Words at once true and kind / Or not untrue and not unkind." Put your character in bed or in another intimate place with her spouse or with another significant character, and let them talk for *two or three pages* about important matters. Here's the catch. No speech of one character can ever answer the speech of the one that goes before it. The characters speak at cross purposes; they have their own agendas. Remember that in conversation, characters also do things. You'll need to know everything about that bedroom or that kitchen before you can write the scene that will be the short-short story.

Writing a Short Story;
Writing a Very Short Story

A world is a bud attempting to become a twig. How can one not dream while writing? It is the pen which dreams. The blank page gives the right to dream.

—GASTON BACHELARD

What You'll Need

GET YOURSELF a good chair. You're going to spend many waking hours sitting in it. You'll want to cushion your butt and support your lower back. I like armrests and wheels. I have a troublesome back (and a chiropractor on call) and when my ship comes in, I'm going to spend $700 on an ergonomic chair, but in the meantime, I go through the thriftier chairs like crazy because one of my cats (I'm not saying which) destroys them.

A desk. My "desks" have included several kitchen tables: enamel, pine, Formica; a wooden TV tray; a glass coffee table; and a hardwood door slab mounted on two sawhorses. These days I've got two proper desks side by side. It takes a lot of room to write a story if you write with a pen as I do, and the cats, of course, need a place nearby to lounge and criticize. I have a friend who sits at a small table at Starbucks every morning with his notebook computer and cup of Pike Place roast and a foot and a half of space and writes all of his novels that way. Not me. My mind does not operate that conveniently. And I find far too many interesting people in there to watch and to eavesdrop on. Virginia Woolf suggested that you may want that desk to be in a room of your own. And when you're in there writing, put up a DO NOT DISTURB sign. Or WRITER AT WORK. Or DANGER: ENTER AT YOUR OWN RISK. My own sign, pilfered from the Hotel Santa Fe, says simply SHH . . .

A pen. Find a favorite. And be sure to have backup. Maybe you prefer a pencil. Get a sharpener; you'll need it. Even if you compose on a computer, you'll need a pen or a pencil or a stylus, perhaps, to make notes, won't you? And you'll need a pen to jot down on a memo pad or on Post-it notes all the intrusive thoughts your practical self uses to lure you away from your writing: *buy milk, call for biopsy results, dentist at 3.* Write it down, forget about it.

My two fingers on a typewriter have never connected with my brain. My hand on a pen does.

A fountain pen, of course. Ball-point pens are only good for filling out forms on a plane.

—*Graham Greene*

Paper. Lined, unlined, blue, white, or yellow—no matter. Buy the paper in bulk—most of it will end up in the trash. I once almost lost a novel when a computer crashed. This was before I knew about the Cloud, or perhaps it happened before the Cloud existed and before I was wise enough to back up my files. I had saved all my handwritten pages and was able to reconstruct and improve on what I had lost.

No distractions. If you're quiet, you will hear the people you've made up talking. Write slowly and rewrite a lot in the early going in order to allow for accidents to happen, for unanticipated characters to stroll onstage, for resonant themes to be discovered. You have to make mistakes to make anything new. Writing a story is taking the path of most resistance. Writing isn't about freedom. Writing creatively is learning to impose limits on your work. Nothing paralyzes the imagination like too much freedom—the tyranny of the blank page. Art is about selection. Art is not life. Life is life. Art is not spontaneous, but premeditated. In order to think of yourself as a fiction writer, imagine yourself as the fiction reader and consider what it is that engages you in a story. What makes you turn the page? I can answer for myself. Intriguing characters, characters I care about and cheer for. New information. I've never been in a world quite like this. A voice I've never heard before. The fresh usual words, one after the other. Surprises. Suspense. Secrets. Vividly rendered and striking details. Seeing my own unarticulated thoughts expressed by the writer.

Inspiration

The familiar definition of inspiration as "divine guidance or influence" seems fanciful, romantic, and false to a writer. We aren't inspired to write. We write and then we are inspired. The muse only comes to the writing desk. She's not hanging out at the pub or in the TV room or at the fabulous party. In other words, you don't wait, you write. Jack London put it very succinctly: "You can't wait for inspiration. You have to go after it with a club."

What is inspiration, after all, but taking in a breath of invigorating air? And to a writer it's knowing what it is you want to write about. It's what happens after you inhale and begin your work. Inspiration is an activity. Waiting for inspiration to arrive is a convenient way to keep yourself from writing and creating. Is that what you want? Inspiration can't be planned for, and it comes out of nowhere, but it arrives only at the writing desk, which is anywhere you are with a pen in your hand. It's what happens when you give your imagination opportunities.

There are many people who want to have written. Writers want to write. We don't have trouble sitting down at the desk. We have trouble getting up from the desk. We do so only when sometimes we have to go find new material or talk to some like-minded folks about writing and literature. On the other hand, inspiration understood as "stimulation of the mind or emotion to a high level of feeling or activity" is crucial to a writer. *Trouble* is inspiration. *Art* is inspiration. When I read a heartbreaking story or listen to sublime music or watch a spellbinding movie, I want to run to the desk and try to shape a story that will enchant and transport my reader in the way I was just transported. *Creating art*, itself, is also inspirational. I see a woman enter my fictional kitchen; I look closely; I see that she has something in her hand; I want to know what it is, I *have* to know, but she won't show it to me; it's her secret, she says. Okay, then, I'll write the scene in which her delicious secret is revealed. And that scene will inspire the next scene, and so on.

The *world* is inspiration. Just this morning I read about a murder in Hawthorne, Florida, a town of fourteen hundred residents in Alachua County. My friend Kim Bradley sent me the link. A fifty-one-year-old man was killed by his nineteen-year-old daughter. The daughter and her mom, the estranged wife of the deceased, decided that with the husband dead they would receive his government benefits, whatever they were. The daughter said she'd do the killing if Mom would drive her to his mobile home. She killed him with a pickax while he slept. After several blows to the head and chest, "The victim continued to make noise so she struck him with the axe until he was quiet to make sure he was dead." The two women cleaned the house and destroyed evidence and then called the police to report finding him dead. Well, I certainly have the trouble I need to start a story. I have the what, now I need the why. Also in the paper this morning, also sent by Kim, and also from Hawthorne, which hasn't seen so much activity since Bo Diddley lived there, a seventy-four-year-old man was mauled by the neighbor's two pit bulls, who tore off one of his arms and nearly severed the other. They chewed through the back of his head. He died at the hospital. Some stories are, as they say, ripped from the headlines.* Fiction writers, however, ask the question many reporters don't: they ask why the person, the owner of the dogs in this case, dogs who had attacked before, did nothing to protect her neighbors or confine her dogs. Fiction writers don't exploit, they explore.

> The object isn't to make art, it's to be in that wonderful state which makes art inevitable.
>
> —*Robert Henri*

Inspiration, like honest emotion, can't be faked. But it can be summoned. It can be cultivated. That's why you keep a notebook with you—to write when you only have a minute. Get rid of your distractions and sit at the writing desk. You're there to think in an unhabitual way. Read a poem. Read a story you love. Put down a word. Any word. And then another. Inspiration appears to the

---

* One need only consider the career of Joyce Carol Oates to realize the significance of a good news story. She wrote *My Sister, My Love*, a novel inspired by the JonBenét Ramsey story; *Zombie*, which seems to have its origin in the Jeffrey Dahmer story; "Where Are You Going, Where Have You Been?" was based on a *Life* magazine article on serial killer Charles Schmid; "Dear Husband" is based on Andrea Yates, the mom who drowned her five children in a bathtub; "Landfill" is based on the tragic death of college student John Fiocco, Jr.; and *Black Water* is based on the death of Mary Jo Kopechne.

attentive and playful mind. The artist Agnes Martin said that inspiration is available to anyone whose mind is not covered over with thoughts and worries. Children have fewer worries than adults and, consequently, more inspiration. We need to think like children. Pablo Picasso put it this way: "It took me four years to paint like Raphael, but a lifetime to paint like a child."

But what to do if you can't get started? First: what not to do. Do not name this temporary condition "writer's block," thereby rendering it legitimate. Know that this lull, this indecision, is an integral part of the writing process. Call it gestation. Remind yourself that the finest work comes from the hardest struggle. Let that sustain you. Write about what's stopping you from writing. If you have an unfinished story in your drawer, and we all do, take it out and work on it. The important thing to know is that when you don't know what to do, do *something*! Like this: Go to Wikipedia and type in *Special:Random*. Write about what your search summons. I just did this search and came up with *David G. P. Taylor*, a British businessman who served as chief executive of the Falkland Islands and later as governor of Montserrat. What I learn immediately is that the executive position in the Falklands was created on the recommendation of Lord Shackleton. I recall the 1982 war over the islands between Argentina and the UK. I remember the 1995 Soufrière Hills volcano that left much of Monserrat uninhabitable. And I learn that Taylor was stationed in Trincomalee, in Sri Lanka, a town I once wrote about in a popular culture paper entitled "On the Road to Trincomalee: The Renaissance of Travel Literature in the United States." Small world. And just like that I've got several possible settings for a story, the themes of exploration, islands, war, and natural disaster. I am reminded that during the Falklands conflict, I attended a Police concert in Boston on April 12, ten days after the war started, where Sting made a comment about British imperialism, and I remember whom I was with, and all that fin de la romance unpleasantness comes rushing back. And I learn a new word, *secondment*, as in, "Taylor went on secondment from Booker . . ." It means "the detachment of a person (such as a military officer) from his or her regular organization for temporary assignment elsewhere." I love learning new words. Then I looked at the ninety or so stunning photographs recently discovered of the ill-fated Shackleton expedition to the Antarctic and the *Endurance* crushed by the ice in the Weddell Sea.

> The impediment to action advances the action. What stands in the way becomes the way.
> —*Marcus Aurelius*

My point is that it may be more important and more valuable to write on those days when, for whatever reasons, the writing is not going smoothly than it is to write on those semi-occasional days when you're firing on all creative cylinders. Anyone can write on a good day. Writers do it every day. You write on the day your cats have spread themselves across all the tablet pages you're trying to write on, and you spill a bottle of Heart of Darkness black ink on the desk while trying to move the hefty one to his perch by the window, and you have to sop up the spill before the cats roll in it, and now you have to wash your hands in Goop, and then you can't find your lucky pen, and the cats let you know with their melodramatic yawns that they couldn't care less, and the phone rings, and it's the roofer about the leak, and every sentence you manage to write seems to plod along like a platoon of undisciplined recruits on a field march. And, of course, the bills are due, and the errands won't run themselves, and the guy next door decides it's time to mow the lawn and fires up his Poulan Pro.

On days like this you need to write and push back against every distraction and every person calling you away from the writing desk. And you don't need discipline to do this; you need love or passion. You're not writing because you have to; you're writing because you want to. Writing is a love of labor as much as a labor of love. Discipline is too much like punishment and rigor and other unpleasantries we'd like to avoid. But we always find time to do the things we love. And when you've finished writing on these difficult days, you've proven to yourself and to the world that you have the grit to be the writer you've always wanted to be, and nothing can stop you now. And then, with the day's work done, then you can engage the so-called real world. But before you do, here's an exercise to get you going.

Dear Abby

John Prine famously wrote a song about "Dear Abby" in which he composed both the letters of distress to Abby and her own practical, sage, and acerbic advice. Now it's our turn to write a very short story in the form of an advice column. I'll write the letter of distress. You write Dear Abby's response.

Dear Abby,

My husband of ten years and I have a very contented and conventional marriage—two kids, one of each, and a Labradoodle—conventional in every way except one. Tom is, I've come to realize, extremely possessive or greedy or selfish or paranoid or all of the above. He writes his name with a permanent black laundry pen on everything he owns. On the handles of his tools, on the backs of framed photographs, on the bottom of chairs, on the cartons of milk in the fridge, and on the peels of his bananas, on anything that he brings into the house. The rest of us are not to touch any of his things. He writes "Tom," not "Tom's," like the objects are extensions of himself. On the soles of his shoes, the waistband of his slacks and his boxers, the inside collar of his shirts, on the Scotch tape dispenser, the lava lamp in the bedroom, on the flat-screen TV, on the patio grill. When I ask him why, he says because. When I say because why, he says because they're mine. Should I ignore Tom's peculiar behavior? I mean, he hasn't written "Tom" on my forehead yet, has he? Or should I ask him to get help for his obsession?

Signed,
Bewildered in Boise

Your very short response in the form of a letter begins with the title "Dear Bewildered," is told in the voice of the advice columnist, and includes enough of the information in the above letter so that your response can stand alone.

The Process

First: Sit Your Ass in the Chair. Sit facing the page. Okay, then. You're at your writing desk, but your central character's at the end of his rope. A desperate man taking desperate measures. You love this guy, but you keep putting obstacles in his way. Writing a story is taking the path of most resistance. So you dip your pen in the ink, and you begin at the edge of the cliff.

You sit at the desk and try to express the inexpressible, try to write those things you cannot say. This makes you anxious. You sense that the only things of value are those that can't be explained but can, you trust, be dramatized. All stories are failures, but you know that a writer is the one not stopped or even fazed by failure. This makes you fearless. Keep in mind what Hecate said in *Macbeth*: "Security is Mortal's chiefest enemy." No art was ever accomplished without risking your neck. You don't know where the story's going, but you trust in the writing process and in your imagination to get you there. You write about what you don't understand. What you don't know is more important than what you do know because what you don't know engages your sense of wonder. You insist on meaning, but not on answers. The point is not to answer, but to question; not to solve, but to seek; not to preach, but to explore. And you believe that life is stranger than fiction because fiction has to make sense.

> It's much easier not to write than to write, unless you're a writer.
>
> —*Elie Wiesel*

A central character wants something intensely and goes after it. As a result of a struggle, he comes to a win or a loss. You take this definition of a plot as a starting point and let the necessary plot do your thinking for you. It will lead you, quite naturally, to considerations of characterization, theme, tone, point of view, setting, and so on. Don't make the plot happen; let it happen. So let's spin out a story by letting the necessary plot lead us on.

You begin, let's say, with a husband and wife, Grady and Alice Bell. You remember Chekhov's advice that *the man and the woman are always the two poles of your story. The North Pole and the South. Every story has these two poles—he and she.* And with the requisite trouble in mind, you open with the death of their child and see if the Bells' marriage can survive this agonizing loss. Their twenty-year-old daughter Hope has died. (You don't need to use an allegorical first name, of course, and you may decide that doing so is a bit heavy-handed, and if so, you'll revise. You're writing a first draft, and not a word is carved in stone.) The Bells are home alone after the funeral and the burial and after the distressing but obligatory reception for family and friends here at the house. Alice is slumped in a corner of the sofa, a sweater draped over her shoulders. She's blotting her swollen eyes with tissues and holding a porcelain teacup in her hand. Grady sits in a ladder-backed chair, elbows on his knees, staring at his folded hands. He believes that if he had been listened to, Hope would still be alive. He wants Alice to accept her responsibility for what happened. And you think, What *did* happen? He says—

In writing a story, you have two choices; you write *scene* or *summary*. You show or tell. Scene reveals; summary explains; scene is intimate and vivid; summary, distant and efficient. Scene is where the writer most directly and most often engages the imagination and the emotions of the reader. And to overstate the point a bit, everything important in a story should be shown, and this looming expression of Grady's resentment is certainly that. You begin as close to Grady's pronouncement as possible. If this is the story of a marriage in trouble, you don't need the years of bliss and prosperity.

> **If you make a scene in the store, you'll be one sorry little boy.**
>
> —*My mother*

Basically scene is this: an uninterrupted unit of dramatic action with a beginning, a middle, and an end. No leaps in time or place. Scene does, however, allow for flashbacks or brief interruptions for memory or reflection. When you write a scene, you're saying this is important—so don't interrupt it, or we'll think it was not important after all. When you want attention, make a scene.

Before you can imagine and write the opening scene, you'll need to look closer at the stage you've begun to set, at the bereaved Bells in their living room, because when people speak, they also do things. Every detail in the room will tell us about the people who live here. Writing a story is archaeology. Spending your time observing your characters, getting to know them intimately, unearthing their secrets, as it were, is an important activity whether you're writing a traditional short story or a short-short story. There is always so much more you have to write than the reader should have to read. You're here to sweat the small stuff. Not all the details in your notes will make it to the page, but, more importantly, each affords you invaluable insight into your characters. The details that do make the page will be those that are both eloquent and consequential. Now you've gotten to know these people better and you feel more confident. You proceed with your scene.

Grady's blue tie—no, his black silk tie—is stuffed into the breast pocket of his suit jacket. He has a scar, you notice, on his left wrist. You know that every scar tells a story. But will this particular story be relevant to yours? You'll find out. He has a milagro, a religious folk charm used for healing purposes, in the shape of an eye, pinned to his lapel. He bought the milagro from a woman outside a church in Chimayo, New Mexico. Grady has, you decide, glaucoma. When he told the woman he also wanted a milagro for his daughter, she said, What's wrong with her? He said, What isn't?

If you hadn't looked closely to try to get to know Grady, you would not have stumbled onto two themes: *vision*—what we see and what we don't; and *healing*. You wonder how you can make these themes resonate. Already you're writing about grief, loneliness, guilt, family, marriage, and death. And you haven't even started. And what did Grady mean by "What isn't?" You want to know, so you write about Hope in your notebook, and you discover that she was a drug addict who'd robbed her parents blind and died of an overdose, alone, in a vacant lot. You had no idea. Back to the living room.

Alice's black hair is cut in bangs, streaked with gray, and held off her face with turquoise barrettes. When the sweater slips off her shoulder, you see that her left arm is tattooed with a flaming heart. On the coffee table there's an emblem of their loss, a photo of baby Hope sitting on a beach blanket, blue floppy hat on her head and zinc oxide on her nose. Beyond Alice you see the staircase that leads to Hope's bedroom. You'll get up there before long to see what clues to Hope's secret life you might uncover.

Under the coffee table is a thread of gold. You see it; the Bells don't. It's a necklace. How might this piece of jewelry play a role later on? Alice rests her teacup on a copy of *Food & Wine*. A sleek black cat sits resplendently atop the bookcase. The potted lilies on the windowsill tell you it's Easter. You note the irony. You can use the season to help set the tone for the story if you wish—and now you have the themes of rebirth and renewal to consider.

Grady reminds Alice that he'd been against throwing Hope out of the house after her last relapse. "You wanted her to hit bottom," he says, "and she did!" Alice feels like she's been clubbed in the face. What does she say or do? You watch her intently with a pen in your hand and you wait. She smashes the teacup, calls Grady a monster. The cat leaps from the bookcase and blasts off into the kitchen. Alice weeps until she can't catch her breath. You write all this down. Grady knows he should go to her, but he's frozen with anger and overcome with shame. Alice heads for the door. Grady tries to stop her. She pushes him away, runs out to the driveway, and screams—the neighbors peek out their open windows. She storms off. Your story is under way.

But whose story will you write? His or hers? *One central character*, remember. Your choice depends on the themes you'd like to explore, on the character who intrigues you more: the one with the most to lose, perhaps. You decide it's Grady's story, and what he wants is to bring Alice home, to heal the wound he has opened, and to repair the damage Hope's addiction and death have done to their marriage. He wants redemption.

Grady's desire to win Alice back must be considerable. Motivation provokes action. So: He loves Alice, can't imagine living without her. He needs her forgiveness, her absolution. Now he has sufficient reason to act. And every time he tries to save the marriage, you'll write a scene. In fact, you might simply proceed by writing these obligatory scenes right up to the climactic moment.

But first you have to decide who's going to tell the story. Grady can tell his story, or a third-person narrator can tell it and grant the reader access to Grady's thoughts and feelings. And maybe to Alice's—you'll see. All first-person narrators are unreliable to some degree because they have a stake in the outcome. If you want Grady's reliability to be a part of your story, you'll let him tell it. If you'd rather focus on his determined struggle to save the marriage, you'll choose a third-person narrator.

So you have a central character, and you know what he wants and why he wants it. Now he has to struggle, as we said earlier, to get what he wants *despite opposition*. Conflict is at the heart of every story. So you leap ahead to that evening when Grady arrives at Alice's sister's condo. He's here to convince Alice to come home. She tells Grady her home was with Hope. He says, You threw her out when she needed us most. Alice says, She was never going to stop as long as she had a safety net. The argument escalates. Grady came to win Alice back, but, instead, drove her further away. He can't stop trying, however, or we have no story. Struggle implies protracted effort, impassioned conflict.

Your next scene: Alice agrees to meet Grady for lunch. They're back to work. He's an admired high school guidance counselor. He's been around troubled kids and has always secretly blamed parents for letting addiction happen to their children. You've just discovered a source of Grady's guilt and his sense of failure. Alice tells Grady she's rented an apartment. He's incredulous. Shouldn't he have known? When Alice comes by to pick up her clothes and some furniture, Grady is helpful and understanding—he's going to take this opportunity to persuade her to stay. She arrives with her pal Austin from the radio station where she works, so Grady never gets a moment alone with her, despite his wrangling, and the whole move is over in twenty minutes.

Grady's obstacle so far has been Alice. Might there be other impediments? You decide to find out. Grady's at his kitchen table poring over photos in the family album trying to discern the moment when his daughter decided, To hell with ballet and tennis; I'm going to be a derelict. His heart is broken. His resolve is wearing thin. Maybe he should let Alice get on with her life, and he with his. There it is! Grady now has to struggle against himself as well. No, he won't let his despair stop him. He calls Alice and leaves a message on her machine. Please, he says, let's try marriage counseling. (And now you've discovered the next scene to write.) He wonders if she's listening to him as he speaks, and so are you. He's wondering if she's alone. You think she's not. The plot thickens.

At counseling, Grady makes it clear he's here to save the marriage. But when Dr. Strout asks Alice what she wants, she says she wants a divorce, a new life. She tells Grady she loves him but can no longer live with him.

The ongoing conflict must be resolved. Grady can fail: Alice moves in with Austin. (You make a note to get to know this guy. He may not be a major character, but he's an important one.) Grady can succeed: Alice comes home. After twenty-two years of marriage, she owes Grady the effort, at least. You'll close with a scene. Here's one possibility: Alice sits on the sofa reading by lamplight, but she's been on the same page for an hour. When Grady looks at her in the light, he sees a halo around her head (his glaucoma). Saint Alice, he thinks. When he notices that the baby photo's not on the coffee table, he realizes Alice is holding the photo behind the book, punishing herself with the image of her loss.

In that moment Grady understands that time will heal some wounds, and he'll eventually get over the loss of Alice, but he also understands that in one case time will make no difference, and he will never recover from the shattering loss of his child. Bringing Alice home has shown Grady the futility of their decision to live together. Your draft's pretty rough, but you'll smooth it out in revision.

Stories aren't written but rewritten, and you have to have something to revise—a complete first draft. The purpose of this draft is not to get it right but to get it written. To err is human, to revise divine. To expect too much from the first draft is to misunderstand the writing process. A good first draft is a failed first draft. If at first you succeed, try, try again. Remember that you can surrender to failure and stop trying (another failure) or you can use the failure to make you brave.

The plot led, you followed, and now you have your causal sequence of events, your essential beginning, middle, and end, and now you go back and add the connective tissue of exposition, flesh out your existing scenes, and write the others you've discovered on the way, like the afternoon outside the church in Chimayo and the night Grady found the necklace he'd given Hope on her sixteenth birthday. And you should do something with Alice's marvelous tattoo. But what? You'll figure it out as you write because your ass is still in the chair, and now you don't want to get up.

You know that you now have enough trouble, enough material, and enough information to write an extensive and textured short story. You've already furnished Alice's sister's condo and Alice's new studio apartment. You've visited the radio station Love 94—Smooth Jazz. You've read most of Hope's sporadic journal entries. You've made notes about Hope's sixteenth birthday party, baked the cake, and written out the invitations. You've been to the churchyard in Chimayo, and gazed into the rheumy brown eyes of the milagro vendor. But you want to write a very short story; you want to capture the essence of the Bells' fall from grace. If a novel is the art of the gaze, and the short story the art of the glance, then the very short story is the art of the glimpse—a gleam or flash of light. And you'll have plenty of raw material to toss away. What you throw away is as important as what you save. You have to have written as much in your notebook for the very short story as for the conventional short story.

Life doesn't come with plots, we're told, except the ones they bury us in. And here's a very short story about just those plots by Leonard Nash.

PLOTS

Your boss, who's got bone cancer, is selling his double-depth burial plot because he's decided to be buried at sea, something about how he'd been a rear admiral in the Navy, or at least that's the word around the office. So this morning you drive to the cemetery with him, and you're excited, because it's the first time you've done anything social together, and that includes riding in the front seat of his new Lexus with its fancy backup cameras and robotic system that parallel parks itself.

You're standing together on the frozen ground under a naked oak tree when your boss says, "I'll bet the view's better from up here."

You laugh at this, but then you remember that the old man is dying. For the first time, you notice that your boss no longer has eyebrows.

So tonight you wipe your lips, satisfied by two helpings of fried lamb chops and microwave mashed potatoes. Your wife's leaning against the water heater when she says, "There's no way I'm going through eternity with you rotting eight inches above me."

"Don't worry," you say. "We'll sign papers so that even if you go first, I'll be placed on the bottom."

Your wife holds a soapy frying pan over her bare feet, the bubbles dripping between her toes and onto the new linoleum you installed some months back when her brother Arthur from Miami (Oklahoma, not Florida) came to town and asked for money again. You backed down, but only after your wife threatened to leave you for good this time. Even so, you insisted that Arthur help you install the new kitchen floor. For weeks the stink of mastic putrefied the air like a spoiled vat of corned beef and sauerkraut.

"Trust me," you tell your wife, "these plots are a terrific deal," but you know she thinks you're full of shit. You'd rather be watching hockey in the living room, but for now you'll settle for poking around in your mouth with your little finger, going after a sliver of meat stuck between your upper molars. Through the kitchen window you can see your neighbor, Richard, trying to jump-start his Winnebago with what looks like a daisy chain of motorcycle batteries. Richard's one of those guys whose garage door is always open while he's out in the driveway fucking around with something.

Two police cars scream past your house and stop at the end of the street. Sure, the neighborhood has changed, but how can you move now, after it took nine months to get a permit for your satellite dish? So you try and score some points by telling your wife you're sorry for everything, and you almost say that you love her, but then she gives you that piercing look you know so well, like she's deciding whether to carve out your heart with the paring knife she's using to peel the red apple she's got. You're hoping she won't start up again about your Internet affair with the actress from Poughkeepsie. Or at least she said she was an actress. For that matter, you hope she was at least a *she*.

When you muster up the courage to leave the room, you stand up from the table, take a toothpick from the pantry, and grab a beer from the refrigerator. For sure, your wife will follow you into the living room, and no doubt there'll be some words, and then tomorrow you'll go in there and apologize to your boss for wasting his time and everything. But first your wife will wait until you're settled into your Stratolounger, watching the Pittsburgh Penguins and the St. Louis Blues on ESPN2. Meantime, your wife turns her back, places the knife into the sink, plops the apple core into the InSinkErator, and while the machine spins and grinds, your wife wipes her feet with a kitchen towel, which she then folds, and rests over the blender like a hat.

———

"Plots" is written in second person point of view, which is unusual enough to always catch the reader's attention, and that's a good thing. Second person works best, I think, in shorter pieces and in present tense, as here. This is a story about social class and humble ambition, among other things. The boss's tricked-out Lexus and his prepaid but superfluous burial plots contrast with our nameless husband's

> Most stories we tell in real life are under 500 words. You're at a party, everyone has a glass of wine, and suddenly you have the floor. You throw out your little story like a grenade.
>
> —*Rebecca Makkai*

domestic details: the exposed water heater in the kitchen, those microwaved potatoes, the linoleum floor, the Stratolounger, and the grinding InSinkErator. Each detail here worth a thousand words. And in the end our unassuming hockey fan's dream of distinction after death is summarily dismissed by his wife, as was his Internet affair with someone who might have been a woman and might have been from Poughkeepsie, the details of which we shudder to imagine.

Leonard's story is a fine example of the use of the objective correlative. Here's how T. S. Eliot defined it: "The only way of expressing emotion in the form of art is by finding an 'objective correlative'; in other words, a set of objects, a situation, a chain of events which shall be the formula of that *particular* emotion; such that when the external facts, which must terminate in sensory experience, are given, the emotion is immediately evoked." Emotion in the writer might not produce emotion in the reader. The writer needs to avoid telling us how to feel and allow us to feel. Here the narrator expresses the character's emotion by showing rather than telling, by evoking the emotion through sensory experiences and details, and by a careful description of the setting.

James Thomas in his introduction to *Flash Fiction* wrote: "Like all fiction that matters, their success depends not on their length, but on their depth, their clarity of vision, their human significance— the extent to which the reader can recognize in them the real stuff of life."

I asked Joe Clifford, editor at *Flash Fiction Offensive*, what he was looking for in the stories he reads: "As an editor, what do I look for? Same as any genre: work that transcends and resonates when I am finished. Anything *can* work, but I've found that the most successful follows the template of (in a concentrated form) 'I/he/she wanted this; I/he/she did that; and here's how it all turned to shit.' Same for any story, regardless of length, I know. But with flash, words are at such a premium, you generally only get a single scene. One POV. It's a snapshot in time with broad, far-reaching ramifications. You can't have a lot of exposition or backstory. Immediate conflict and establishing what's at stake. Get in, get out. Of course, I work in crime."

The hallmarks of short-shorts are brevity, intensity, and perhaps unexpectedness. There are fewer words in a short-short, and so every word is more important. Flash fictions are sleek and efficient machines. Mood or tone may carry more weight than in traditional stories because there is less time to exploit plot or examine and develop character. Mood might evoke what plot could show. Make your title do its work, let it grab the reader by the shirt collar and say, "You have to read this story! It's only going to take a minute!" Start in the middle of things. Focus on one or just a few characters. Write long and then trim. Let the last line be your best line. Don't write beyond it. You want that line to resonate in the reader's mind when she puts down the story. Your job is to entertain, to provoke thought and engage emotions. If it's emotionally powerful, the reader will finish the story. And it might be a good idea to put one very powerful image in your story. Or two. As in this story by Bonnie Losak.

FLOOR TWELVE—PEDIATRIC PSYCH UNIT

In Bed 1, Sumner is curled into the shape of a capital C. Next to her, in the bed by the window flanked with metal bars, Aubrey drifts in and out of sleep. Sumner's right arm is wrapped in a beige elastic bandage that starts below the knuckles and edges up toward the elbow. The bandage is partially hidden under a blue fabric sling. According to her chart, Sumner shoved her fist through an awning window that was nailed shut. I don't believe that skinny fourteen-year-old really punched through a window, but I'm only the nurse's assistant. Folks don't ask my opinion. Besides,

Aubrey takes up most of my time in Room 1205. She's always vomiting and then there's the cleanup and the fight to try to get her to drink some of that nasty orange Pedialyte to make up for the fact that she doesn't seem to be able to keep anything down.

Aubrey's stepmom came to visit yesterday. She sat on Aubrey's bed, wrinkled up her forehead, and forced a few tears out. Then she dabbed at her cheeks real ladylike. I watched Aubrey to see if those fake tears would get a reaction. But she wasn't fooled. Not Aubrey. Aubrey took one look at her stepmom's plastered-down hair and barely-wet cheeks, and pulled the blankets up under her chin. Then she squeezed her eyes shut. Wouldn't open them even when her stepmom called her name and shook at her shoulders. Finally, that lady just clucked her tongue against her teeth and headed out. After the door whined shut I whispered that Aubrey's visitor had gone, like I wasn't even talking to Aubrey or anything. Just talking to myself, that's all. Aubrey opened her eyes, squinting-like. She peered around and then lowered the blankets a bit. I nodded at Aubrey and, after considering me for a moment, she nodded back. It was just a slight shift in her chin, quick but deliberate. Not much of a connection, but up here on the twelfth floor, sometimes it's all we get.

———————

Sumner curled in the bed like capital C for *Catatonic*; her arm swaddled in a beige elastic; Aubrey's fake tears, that clucking tongue; those eyes squeezed defiantly shut, and the unexpected connection between Aubrey and our otherwise ignored narrator, she who has told us this story of desperate children in such a matter-of-fact tone of voice that we can take it all in calmly and utter a small cheer of relief when our nurse's aide announces Aubrey's temporary freedom.

Like all fiction, the very short story is about people, and it strives to tell us what it's like to be a human being and how that feels. The very short story needs to be compelling, needs to engage the reader emotionally, needs to take us out of our world and drop us into the world of the story, and ought to tell us something we don't know about ourselves. It might be funny or unsettling. It should provoke us, change our lives, break our hearts, or stun us with insight. Like this short-short by Steve Almond in which our author performs a feat of redemptive magic.

NIXON SWIMS

This is in '73, late, a last surge of autumn. We're in Tacoma, a publicity tour to honor some dam demolished to save Indians. Watergate is unraveling faster and faster and my boss, Richard Nixon, has become a fierce shadow in a festering suit.

Our helicopter lands and someone from Interior leads us to the riverbank, where the tribal rep explains about salmon and the necessity of strong water. The chief appears, solemn, corpulent, reeking of peppery cologne. He leads Nixon to a step pool and points out the fish: giant, shimmering pelts. Resting for the rapids, the chief explains.

Back at the chopper the reporters have marshaled

themselves, prowling in cuffed trousers, tapping their pads. But Nixon stays a bit longer. Some little Indian kids sing to him and he asks one, "Are you happy to have your river back?"

The girl nods.

"Show me," he says. "Show me how the salmon swim." And when she does he imitates her, his crabbed shoulders rising. Soon all the children are swimming like salmon, rushing to make more of themselves against the ancient, expected forces. The sun shows no signs of leaving. The river, wishing only to be left alone, whispers past. This is Richard Nixon recognizing one good thing and by so doing canceling every bad. This is grace, a kind of unintended forgiveness.

Occupations

When we were teenagers hanging out in front of Denholm's department store on Main Street, my friends and I played a game that I always thought of as "Occupations," though we never called it anything. We'd watch people walk by, and we'd suggest to each other what this or that person did for work. The clothes, the walk, the gear, the hair, the eyes gave us our clues. It was never enough to say "lawyer." We needed to be specific: "Handles real estate transactions for the Catholic diocese, processes evictions . . ." From the occupation we'd build a narrative by adding details of the subject's life, quickly before he rounded a corner or entered a building and before the next, more interesting figure walked by. Like this for our real estate lawyer: His wife, Mary Kathleen, doesn't know about the new secretary, and if Phil can help it, she never will. Not until he's had his chance with this Kelly O'Brien at the regional conference in Hyannis next month. He's got two boys at St. John's, both on the crew team, both going to be lawyers like the old man. His brother, John-Joe, Father John-Joe, S.J., is an alcoholic, but he's tucked away in a small parish in Athol, thank God.

So try this. Go to a restaurant or a bar and get a table where you can linger and observe. Look at the diners and drinkers. Imagine what they do, what the home lives are like, what they are talking about, and so on. Just write about these interesting characters who have the benefit of appearing before you with physical descriptions and clothes, but with new, richly textured lives. Imagine what they do for work. Imagine how their jobs define them. Watching flesh-and-blood people is better than watching the TV people that someone else made up. And now write your short-short story.

And here's a story by Debra Monroe that is rife with strangeness and vivid images, and longing and loss and humor about a self-employed man whose occupation is collecting.

TRANSIT (1986)

I towed my worldly goods to a remote plot with real snakes in the grass, real primroses near pathways, and I wasn't a tisket-a-tasket girl running errands but an adult with a narrow skill set that had sent me toward serial opportunities, jobs, my career not careering but ascendant as I checked off items on widely circulated how-to lists, but no one could tell me how to succeed at love. People who hired me knew previous people who'd hired me, and my reputation grew, good at work, bad at love. Portents. Omens. Would I get some? I'd been too picky, a vague voice on the phone, my father's, said. Eavesdropping, I heard, not meant for me, about me, my supervisor describing me: *otherwise intelligent with unaccountably odd taste in men.* Amused at his succinctness, I took to introducing myself this way, but no one could handle irony, the locals literal, my effect caustic. I explained it: the adjacency of deliberately opposite things. I stayed matchless but ordinary, billing-and-cooing-to-no-avail. A condition so common then that *Newsweek* declared women my age more likely to be killed by terrorists than locate love.

Everyone gets three wishes, I believed, and I stood outside and thought, don't hunt, just wait, and the stars shone as I heard rustling, footfalls on sere leaves, deer foraging, and the next night at a wild party a man asked three times if I liked ballads. I said: No. No. No. Also: Why do you ask that over and over? Our conversation waltzed, a cadence. He said, "Feisty. I like it." He tracked me down with his wishing-well eyes, his limpid eyes, eyes of a newfound familiar. He was here, now, native. My irony flew out the window and away. I settled. (*What links them in nature? An instant of blind rut.* James Joyce.) I'd hoped for a mutual something else too, but no. Nil. Squat. Beans. He started buying Airstream trailers, Airstream trailers sprouting tubular across green acres. He'd inherited land, houses. Yet he slept in the Airstreams, an investment, he said, their value going up, up, and he'd likely recoup, but for now he wanted to sleep in a different one every night.

He spent princely sums on AMC Pacers and parked them too. He said, "I had a dream I was driving to California in one, and California seemed like the future, so I invested." My heart lurched hopeful because he believed in signs, in stood-fors, in metaphors, so we had that in common. But such useless stood-fors, I conceded next, this collecting jones so harebrained and cockeyed, so loony, I couldn't pretend he was bright in his own field, his own field filling with rusty trailers and cars. He said, "A friend asked me why, and I gave him the same answer, that I'd dreamed I was driving to California in an AMC Pacer, and this was a sign the car was my future, and my friend said, 'Fool. The dream meant you move to California.'" So said *my* investment, my used-to-be quest's end, also "Ha ha," because he, unlike me, didn't mind a wrong turn leading to a good last line. I'd been led here, to this temporary alignment, he dreaming himself somewhere but staying still, and I was revving up but wishing myself still, deep-rooted. No magic. No magic. I didn't stay.

———————

Maybe the point of a story is to replace confusion with meaning. After all, nothing is as boring or so maddening as confusion. Someone learning something new turns an event into a story.

A Formal Feeling Comes

Fiction is experimentation; when it ceases to be that, it ceases to be fiction.

—JOHN CHEEVER

OTHER THAN the somewhat loose length restrictions, the form of the very short story is open to exploration and experimentation. You are, in fact, helping to define or describe the genre as you write. Think of your literary experiment as a trial, an innovation, an unconventional and novel scheme for the purpose of discovering something previously unknown, unsaid, and unfamiliar, something that could not be achieved by writing in a nonprovocative traditional form, let's say. This experiment must, however, be grounded in some conventions. You'll use words, of course, arranged in sentences, to address the human condition. People are always the focus and concern of fiction. To echo Cheever, when people cease being the subject of stories, people will cease reading stories. The form is open, and a nontraditional and unorthodox form might, in fact, lead you to your material. And that's what we'll investigate in this chapter—formal experimentation. Anton Chekhov wrote stories in a number of unusual forms, including diary excerpts, lists of math problems, lonely hearts ads, legal depositions, and homework assignments. Peter Constantine, a translator of Chekhov, writes that when Anton was a medical intern, his autopsy reports read like stories. Let's consider using some "found forms" to construct our very short stories. And why don't we start with a familiar form to most of us, the homework assignment.

My Summer Vacation

Your narrator is an innocent, a child of six or seven. He or she has had a thrilling and joyous summer holiday and has listed all the wonderful activities and the friends and family who shared the holiday. At the shore, maybe. In the mountains or a forest. In tents, in cabins, in motels. The narrator will sign his or her report, so be sure to give him or her a name. We can feel the child's excitement and delight, but beneath the narrative we sense something else, something the child is unaware of, something darker, something ominous and alarming. Your job is to insinuate the menace into the child's cheerful composition.

> You can't create unless you're willing to subordinate the creative impulse to the constriction of form.
>
> —*Anthony Burgess*

And here's an extended assignment for your Spring Break.

The Un-New

Go to a flea market or thrift store and buy any used object that catches your eye and engages your imagination. Study it; clean it; place it by your desk and admire it. Write about it. Take a photo of it. Describe it in as much detail as you can. Tell the story through its imagined provenance: Who are all the people who owned it? Why did they get rid of it? Did they lose it? How did it end up at the flea market? The story is about the person or people you discover, not the object itself. Objects provoke stories. Write the story in five hundred words.

A word about description before we move on. Naming is not describing. Brand names, for example, do not let us see the object, although they might indicate a character's superficiality, and their inclusion in your story might be purposeful. Writers need to know the names of things, but even the names of things might not be enough. Let's say you have a cat in your story, not unlike the cat lying on my notes as I type this. The word *cat* is not much of a description, even though it does give us a general idea of the inscrutable critter in the room. There are fifty-eight breeds of cat, just for starters, recognized by the International Cat Association. But what is a cat? Well, according to Linnaean taxonomy, a cat is a being whose cells have nuclei, who is not a plant, has a spine and hair, provides milk for its young, and eats meat. But that's still not helping us see the beast. So we extend the taxonomy. Cochise, we see, is a brindled Maine coon with blue eyes, a silky grayish coat, white neck and paws, who chirps when he sees a squirrel and picks up his food with his nimble paw one kibble at a time. You can see him better now.

———

And let's move on to the end of life with obituaries. An obituary is the record of a death and necessarily contains a reference to the life. It usually includes mentions of the full name of the deceased, including maiden names and nicknames; birthplace;

> The great thing about form
> is that it hinders us from
> saying what we had originally
> intended to say.
>
> —John Glenday

family, including parents, children, grandchildren, and those predeceased; friends; pets; education; military service; occupation; hobbies; achievements; anecdotes; cause of death. (And it gives rise to the wonderful adverb *obituarily*, meaning "in the manner of an obituary; posthumously," and the adjective *obituarial*, meaning "in the manner of an obituary," not to mention *obituarian*, which you'll be in the following exercise, and *obitual*, relating to a person's death). An obituary is an attempt to give an account of the texture and the significance of the life of someone who has recently died. So write an obit— maybe your own—and try to suggest the public and private life of the deceased and bring in his or her world and his or her vision.

By way of example, here's an excerpt from an obituary in the *Medford Mail*, February 4, 1904, on the passing of one William Plymale.*

> *This week we regret to announce the death of W. J. Plymale, of Jacksonville, who has been a resident of Jackson*

* Errors uncorrected.

County for over fifth years. Mr. Plymale died on Sunday evening, at his home in Jacksonville, after a short illness from pneumonia, at the age of sixty-six years, eleven months and one day.

Mr. Plymale was born in Knox county, Tennessee, February 9, 1837, and came to Oregon with his parents in 1851, arriving in Jackson County in November of that year. The family settled on what is yet known as the Plymale place, and Mr. Plymale received his early education at Jacksonville, afterward attending the Willamette University at Salem.

He first engaged in farming in this county, which occupation he followed for over twenty years. In 1876 he sold his interest in the farm and moved to Jacksonville, where he has since resided. . . .

Mr. Plymale was a man of strong convictions, and excellent traits of character. Thoroughly honest and up right, his influence in affairs in this country has been a marked one, and always for the public good. In the early sixties he was married to Miss Josephine Martin, a member of another pioneer family, and a woman of more than ordinary literary and social gifts. From this marriage twelve children were born, one of whom died in childhood.

A man of considerable heft in a community that values its history and traditions. Mr. Plymale is praised with abstractions: "strong convictions" and "excellent traits of character." Not everyone who dies, of course, is a pillar of the community. Here's another newspaper obit from July 22, 1871.

Ashbach *Dead—a German laborer named Ashbach, employed on the two-story brick building near the Union*

School House, fell from the roof to the ground on Friday last, injuring him fatally—he died that night.

Not even a first name. No history. No praise. Not all obituaries need to be as sober as those above. Consider these two obituary excerpts from my hometown paper:

"She enjoyed shopping, doing crossword puzzles, cooking, popping bubble wrap and collecting angels."

Of a school custodian:

"He enjoyed painting parking lot lines with his best friends Vin and Rich."

From such small but revelatory details are fully imagined characters built. An obituary's tone might be uncomplaining:

"So . . . I was born; I blinked; and it was over. No buildings named after me; no monuments erected in my honor."

It might be humorous, as this excerpt about the death of a fifty-three-year-old man of natural causes:

"He was sadly deprived of his final wish, which was to be run over by a beer truck on the way to the liquor store to buy booze for a date."

Here's another death by "natural" causes:

"It is believed it was caused from carrying her oxygen tank up the long flight of stairs to her bedroom that made her heart give out. She left behind a hell of a lot of stuff to her daughter and sons who have no idea what to do with it."

One might use a parent's obituary to settle a family score:

"At the time of her death, Dot was visiting her daughter, Carol in Memphis. Carol and her husband, Ron, away from home attending a "very important conference" at a posh Florida resort, rushed home 10 days later after learning of the death."

The Dead Beat

Now is your chance to write an obituary that is also a very short story. You might want to read obituaries in newspapers or check in with the website of the Society of Professional Obituary Writers for some suggestions and examples. London's *Daily Telegraph* has the best obits, in my opinion. This can be funny, ironic, sad, whatever you feel. Consider the life of your character and any struggles that he or she may have had. Did that struggle lead to the death? Consider the subject's public life and his or her private life. Consider who is writing the obituary. A devoted child? A loving spouse? The newspaper's obituary writer? What does the writer bring of himself or herself to the narrative?

Now, how about a very short story in the style of a wedding announcement? Announcements often mention the names of the bride and groom, their residence, their occupations, mention the parents and grandparents, and might include honeymoon plans. Here's a terse, vintage newspaper announcement:

Miss Mary Jane Livingston of this city and the Rev. Thomas Brown of Morgan City, were married on the 16th at the residence of the bride's mother. A number of friends of the contracting parties were present, who, in conjunction with numerous acquaintances, wished the newly wedded pair all the joys of felicity.

Old, New, Borrowed, and Blue

So your job is to make up a couple who are getting married and want the world to know it. Name them. Give them parents, step-parents, grandparents. Find out where they live. Assemble the bridal party; design the wedding gown; send out invitations; go to the rehearsal dinner; select the church; choose the music; let the ceremony begin; host the reception, and write the wedding announcement that will be your very short story.

Here's a short-short story by Steve Almond that plays with this idea:

ANNOUNCEMENT

Congratulations to Hector and Consuelo Acuña on the engagement of their daughter, Felicidad, who they never thought would amount to much of anything and secretly feared would return home pregnant from one of her many sweaty summer dates with Ronny Hask, a near graduate of Weed Senior High, who dreams of being a pilot for a small airline someday if he can overcome his vertigo. The couple plan an October wedding at St. Sebastien's (assuming construction of the new rectory is complete) with reception to follow at Red's Marathon Lodge.

The Hask family, natives of nearby Hudspeth, will sponsor a rehearsal dinner at The Pasta Factory, where the two families will make loud inappropriate remarks about the couple and, more softly, about one other.

Consuelo will cry most of the afternoon, because Felicidad is her only daughter after four Acuña boys (may they each find peace) and because they love one another so much they once fought with butter knives in the dinette area. Ronny's mother, Dee, will also tear up, though in private, because that is how things are done in her family.

Let God watch over this young pair as they lie vibrating with desire and wake damp and foul in their mouths and later, after they have moved on to another town, mugged of their naïveté, and all their lives seem a struggle to stand under the weight of what they have done, and what has been done to them, let God still watch.

Let's consider writing a bit of flash fiction modeled on a diary and/or a journal entry or entries. And let's distinguish between them. We'll begin with the diary. Here we have a person talking to himself or herself. We talk to ourselves before we talk to the world. Some of us do anyway. A diary is a way to remember. It's a place to articulate and store your nightly dreams. It's a way to share a secret without giving the secret away. A diary entry is a confession. It's a reminder of the importance of our daily lives. It encourages us to be mindful. Louis Menand wrote about diaries in the *New Yorker*: "It's not that we imagine that we would be happier if we kept a diary; we imagine that we would be better— that diarizing is a natural, healthy thing, a sign of vigor and purpose, a statement, about life, that *we care*, and that non-diarizing or, worse, failed diarizing is a confession of moral inertia, an acknowledgement, even, of the ultimate pointlessness of one's being in the world." He goes on to suggest that people for whom the diary is ego-driven will not keep going because the level of vanity and self-importance demanded in the endeavor is too great. People who use diaries to record wishes and desires that they need to keep secret and to list fears and failures they cannot admit to publicly will also stop writing because what they really want to do is to forget. But before they do, they might reveal more of themselves than they know. Like this partial entry from the diary of a heroin addict:

> Form is a straitjacket in the way that a straitjacket was a straitjacket for Houdini.
>
> —*Paul Muldoon*

"*December 29, 1986: I've been thinking about last Christmas Eve when I picked up that girl in a strip club, brought her back here on my bike, took her home the next day, then had Christmas dinner all by myself at McDonald's. I haven't made much progress I see.*"

If you're like me, you wish he'd written about McDonald's on the Christmas afternoon. A story there certainly. That excerpt is from *The Heroin Diaries: A Year in the Life of a Shattered Rock Star* by Nikki Sixx.

A third motivation for writing a diary is to write it for someone else—there is a reader in mind. And maybe this is the diary most worth reading (and writing, in our specific case). Several years ago I found a fifty-four-page diary on eBay with the provocative caption: "Handwritten Diary Pregnancy, Love, Cheating and Suicide." The diary was written by a teenage girl in Louisiana who fell in love with one teenage boy and had a baby with another. The diary entries, which spanned seven months, told her story. The first entry begins with an announcement of her pregnancy, a mention of her parents' distress, her own happiness, and her plans to marry when she turns eighteen. But then she is ridiculed at school. She quits school when she's six months "prego." Her boyfriend goes to jail after a fight with the other boy, and then, "This has been the worst week of my life." Our diarist reports that she had the baby, but based on the date of the delivery, the father could not have been the boyfriend. But the boyfriend comes through and says he'll marry her.

Folded into the diary, along with the diarist's photograph, is a suicide letter in the form of a poem which begins: "Living a life of madness truly in dismay."

The most famous diarist in the English language is Samuel Pepys. He wrote it in the strictest secrecy; even his friends did not know of its existence. To preserve his secret, he wrote the diary in the shorthand called tachygraphy, but this was so complicated he quickly devised his own shorthand system. Even so, his diary consisted of 3,000 quarto-sized pages, which Pepys had bound in six leather volumes. When it was finally transcribed in the nineteenth century, 1.3 million words covered 9,325 pages and filled fifty-six volumes. Pepys, who publicly was a great moralist, was a secret lecher, but because he kept no secrets from his diary, it so shocked the publisher that the first edition was heavily bowdlerized.

Oct. 25, 1666: And at night W. Batelier comes and sups with us; and after supper, to have my head combed by Deb, which occasioned the greatest sorrow to me that ever I knew in this world; for my wife, coming up suddenly, did find me imbracing the girl con my hand sub su coats. . . .

*I wast at a wonderful loss upon it, and the girl also; and I
endeavoured to put it off; but my wife was struck mute and
grew angry, and as her voice came to her, grew quite out
of order; and I do say little, but to bed; and my wife said
little also, but could not sleep all night; but about 2 in the
morning waked me and cried.*

Diaries that look out at the world tend to be more interesting
to read than the navel-gazing sort. Virginia Woolf kept a diary.
Here's an entry from July 23, 1930:

*Edith Sitwell has grown very fat, powders herself thickly,
gilds her nails with silver paint, wears a turban & looks
like an ivory elephant, like the Emperor Heliogabalus.* I
have never seen such a change. She is mature, majestical.
She is monumental. Her fingers are crusted with white
coral. She is altogether composed.*

Woolf wrote what most of us would call a journal or a writer's
notebook, rather than a diary. In fact, she called hers "Holdalls."
Like diaries, journals are about memories and mindfulness. But a
journal is not a daily record of occurrences. A writer's diary might
have the same entry every day: *Sat down to write at 9. Stopped at
8, had a drink, read, and went to sleep.* We don't lead eventful lives
except for those lives in our heads. The notebook is not meant
to be an obsession, but a tool. Journal writers are not interested
in facts, per se, but in stimulation. The notebook is not so much
about what happened, as about what could happen. A notebook

---

* Marcus Aurelius.

is a reminder that you're a writer and that what you're currently doing while you're out of the house, away from the desk, is taking notes toward your next story or novel. You know that you think differently when you have a pen in your hand—and you observe differently. You see what's really there, not what's supposed to be there. You keep a notebook to teach yourself to pay attention. You keep a notebook to encourage yourself to create. A notebook or journal is a warehouse, not a museum.

Dear Diary

Write your short-short story in the form of a diary entry or a series of entries or as a journal entry or entries. Perhaps an entry by a character you make up. Or a character you borrow from history or from fiction. Raskolnikov's diary? The diary of the woman moneylender he killed? Holden Caulfield's journal? That waitress who smiled at you this morning? What secrets is she keeping in that diary?

According to *Larousse Gatronomique*, the first restaurant, as we know them now, opened in Paris in 1765 on what is now the Rue du Louvre, when a man named Boulanger, who made bouillon, put on his sign "Boulanger sells restoratives fit for the gods." We can imagine that the first restaurant reviews soon followed. In fact, Denis Diderot said of Boulanger's establishment that "one was well but expensively fed." Generous sentiments from the guy who also said this: "Man will never be free until the last king is strangled with the entrails of the last priest." The first *New York Times* restaurant review, by an anonymous reporter, appeared in 1859, and had this to say about a third-class eating house on Water Street: "The smell peculiar to this establishment does not partake of the spices of Araby the Blest; the principal odor being rather ammoniacal in its character, and suggestive of stables."

> Everything can have drama if it's done right. Even a pancake.
>
> —*Julia Child*

These days, websites like Open Table, Zagat, and Yelp have allowed us all to be restaurant critics or pundits no matter the discernment of our palates. Here are a few excerpts from online reviews, all uncorrected:

> We split King crab legs and for 55 bucks a lb I think they could of been warmer and came with warm drawn butter but nope potato was cold carrots were dry And cold.

> The whole experience was almost like being at a friend's home for dinner (except you got a bill at the end).

> I would rather pass kidney stones without pain medication than be dragged here again.

> At some point our waiter, Bucci, who has been studiously avoiding us, tells us that there are items you can order that are not on the menu, but you have to know about them.

And there are the more astute professional reviewers, who can be as caustic:

If Villard Michel Richard doesn't make it as a restaurant, it could reopen as the Museum of Unappetizing Brown Sauces. —Pete Wells, *New York Times*

It's worth going to see what the unmitigated male ego looks like, when expressed as a restaurant. —Jay Rayner, *Guardian*

Gastronomy

So now you'll write a story in the form of a restaurant review. Read some, of course, to get the feel of the genre. There are thousands online. But we're here for the characters and the story, more than the food itself. So remember to use your five senses, which might be easier to do in a restaurant than anywhere else. For *taste* you might mention the incendiary ghost pepper cracker bombs; for *smell* maybe the perfume of bouquet in your potato leek soup; for *hearing* either the blare of TVs or the serenity of a Mozart string quartet over the sound system; for *touch* the texture of the linen napkin or the mouthfeel of the sprouted wheat bread; and for *seeing*, how about the caviar amuse, which seems to be levitating on a cloud of smoke over a glass column. Tell us who you're with; tell us what the trouble is.

Suddenly in eighth grade, arithmetic was replaced with the soon-to-be-discredited-but-not-discredited-soon-enough-for-me New Math, and that's when the worlds of mathematics and literature collided, and I wasn't wearing a seat belt. We were soon asked to solve word problems. Until then I hadn't considered words as problems, but as friends and allies. You know the word problems I mean:

Brock's profit for February was $550.50 and was 13% lower than his profit in January. What was his January profit?

Or:

If every day you walk six miles in one hour and fifty minutes and your friend Chris walks eight miles at the same pace, how long will it take Chris to walk his eight miles?

Sister Dominic Marie wanted answers. I wanted stories. What was Brock's business? Was anyone subverting him at work? Why doesn't Chris want to walk with me? Sister wanted proof. I wanted mystery. How do I really know if Chris is walking those extra miles?

So let's try writing a very short story as a word problem, which is also called a story problem. You might even make a quadratic equation the title of the story. Solve for X, and all that. There are distance problems, age problems, work problems, percentage problems, mixture problems, and number problems.

Here's one written in jest by Gustave Flaubert:

Since you are now studying geometry and trigonometry, I will give you a problem. A ship sails the ocean. It left Boston with a cargo of wool. It grosses 200 tons. It is bound for Le Havre. The mainmast is broken, the cabin boy is on deck, there are 12 passengers aboard, the wind is blowing East-North-East, the clock points to a quarter past three in the afternoon. It is the month of May. How old is the captain?

Solve for X

Time to write your own very short story as a word problem. Get out your old math textbooks and read a few before you start. Consider quantities, mathematical language, variables, measurements, relationships, and structure. Find yourself a central character who has a barrel of grapes or is on a bus traveling at warp speed or is selling gift wrap for a class trip or has one fistful of pencils costing 13 cents each and another fistful of erasers costing 8 cents each. Ask yourself, what is her problem? What is on his mind? Calculate what might happen.

I couldn't resist doing one myself.

WORD PROBLEM

The North Shore Limited pulls out of Westland Station at 7:25 a.m., heading for Eastland, 263 miles away, traveling at 67 mph, which is not nearly fast enough for Trent X, who is sitting in the dining car, sipping his tepid coffee, and staring at the appalling ugliness of the desolate prospect out his window, every brownfield and every dilapidated house a lacerating insult to his sensibilities. He shuts his eyes and imagines Kathy's delight when he shows up at her condo today, unannounced, and asks her to marry him. At 8:13 a.m.. Kathy Y leaves Eastland Station aboard the Lakeshore Zephyr, headed for Westland, traveling at 61 mph on a track parallel to the North Shore Limited's, making one 5-minute stop at mile 45 in Blisterville. She's distracting herself with a crime novel set in Las Vegas, but it's not working. She imagines how flabbergasted Trent will be when she arrives at his flat unannounced and how despondent he'll be when she calls off the romance, breaks his heart. At Blisterville, Tonio K boards the train and takes a seat beside his new girlfriend Kathy. They embrace and Tonio tells her everything will be all right. He hopes he made the terms of their affair clear enough. He is who he is, after all. Can a leopard change his spots? At what time will the trains meet, and when they do, when the dozing Trent is slapped out of dreamland by the concussion of colliding slipstreams, will he look out the window and see a woman with her head resting against her own window, a woman who looks very much like Kathy, but can't be? And will Kathy feel the vibration of the train in her skull and in her teeth and visualize the coming unpleasantness with Trent and the ensuing, redemptive bliss with Tonio? And since the two envisioned visitations will not, in fact, happen, can this relationship between Trent and Kathy be saved? Everything happens for a reason. Isn't that what they say? Show your work.

———————

Let's try a story inspired by and in the form of a personals ad. A person is looking to attract a lover and does so publicly if discreetly. As with all narrative, the first line is the most important—you're trying to attract an eye that's speeding down a column of print. The writer wants to say something about herself and about the sort of person she's looking for. And somewhere in there must be the outcome the writer desires. Personals ads have been around for quite a while. Here's one taken from a nineteenth century newspaper:

A young lady, country bred, but easily tamed and civilized, would like to correspond with a city gentleman, with a view to matrimony. It is necessary for him to be wealthy, and not less than forty years of age, as she would "rather be an old man's darling than a young man's slave." The advertiser is 21, and presumes her manners and appearance will recommend her to tastes not overly fastidious; also a lady of position, and will expect replies from responsible parties only; therefore, triflers, take heed. Address Matilda, station D, Post office.

Consider where it is you're placing the ad. If your ad is running in the *New York Review of Books*, you might be looking for an accomplished, intellectually inclined, retired professor for a lasting and mutually caring relationship. If your ad is on Craigslist, you might not be so fussy, and if you're a woman, you might include a list of traits you're looking for:

1. At least five feet ten and not a porker
2. Takes care of themselves
3. Mad about SEC football (but not the Gators)
4. Not a cheater
5. Enjoys a little afternoon delight
6. Likes to watch *Hoarders*
7. Not married
8. Doesn't mind if I get bitchy you know when
9. Has most of his teeth
10. Wants in for the long haul

And so on. You might even include deal-breakers like, "No hitting on my sister."

Getting Personal

Now it's your turn to write a very short story in the form of a personals ad. So: Who are you? Where are you? How old are you? Who are you looking for? How can you appeal to the person of your dreams? What do you want from him or her? Who will you be sending the ad to? Do it in three hundred words.

How To

The process essay explains how to do something or explains how something works. It's also called the do-it-yourself essay or the how-to essay. And it's pretty straightforward. You'll introduce the process you're going to explore and then the reader will often simply follow the steps to completion to accomplish the task you're explaining, or she will at least understand the process. Be sure to mention things that can go wrong and to mention the tools and supplies needed if appropriate. And, of course, you're telling a story. For brilliant examples of the process essay as fiction, read Lorrie Moore's collection *Self-Help*.

Here's a very short story by Mary Slebodnik.

HOMETOWN MARKET'S
DELICIOUS FRIED CHICKEN
SERVES: ANYONE WILLING TO PAY $23.00 A BOX
($11.99 AFTER 7:00 P.M.)

1. Tie the apron. Stretch your fingers into the plastic gloves. Go to the cooler, that dark cell filled with raw meat in the back of the grocery store, and pull the chicken out of the cardboard boxes. Count the wings, breasts, and thighs—shapes you have memorized—and drop them into the green bucket. The cold chicken blood numbs your fingers through the gloves. Distract yourself by humming along to the chorus of the song playing over the intercom: "If I Had a Million Dollars."

2. Haul the bucket to the sink and wash each piece of chicken. Roll the chicken around in the silver tub of seasoned flour and begin daydreaming about your Great American Novel, but become distracted by what you would do with a million dollars instead. You find yourself wanting to sit somewhere French with a typewriter while wearing a smoking jacket.

3. Turn on that monster, the fryer: a big vat of boiling vegetable oil. Make sure it's hot. The last time you cooked, you put the chicken in too early, and the breading got all slippery and slimy, the pieces hanging in lukewarm oil, suspended—chicken in purgatory. Be kind to the chicken. Give it no hope of survival.

4. Drop the chicken piece-by-piece into the fryer. (Of course, you will need to have lowered the wire basket into the grease first. If you did not do this step, grab a set of tongs from under the deli counter and fish the chicken out before it burns on the hot coils. That's what happens when chicken has the freedom to do whatever it wants.)

5. Notice that you didn't put on the apron referred to in step one. Your belly has a certain prominence and somehow you can never keep it out of the flour. Put on the apron now so Jake the Adorable Stockboy won't see your gut covered in bleached wheat. He calls you Fitzgerald because he knows your literary ambitions. Wave to him when he makes his 9:00 a.m. appearance with the milk stacked on a pushcart.

6. Set the timer for the chicken.

7. Stir the chicken halfway through its cooking time with a giant metal spatula to keep the pieces from sticking together. This will be around the time Jake comes over to flirt with you. Ask him what he would do with a million dollars.

8. When Jake says he would buy a boat, explain that a million dollars would buy far more than a boat. Do not betray your disappointment when he says he'll buy a "big boat."

9. When you realize you forgot to set the timer (like last time), take the chicken out and poke it with a thermometer. If you can poke through the breading without too much trouble, put the burnt chicken in the case and sell as much

as you can before your manager comes back. If you have to unduly exert yourself to stab through the breading, throw the chicken away. Cover it in the wastebasket with paper towels. Pretend it never happened. Do steps 1–4 again.

10. When a customer calls, ask her, "What would *you* do with a million dollars?" When she says, "Oh, no! I just wanted the deli people," reassure her and jot down her order.

11. Go to the cooler with two green buckets so you can accommodate the caller's request for 39 skinless chicken breasts for her family reunion. Tear off the skin, and toss the chicken into the flour.

12. Don't want more. Don't ever want more.

———————

The young writer pays her dues with a mind-numbing day job in this delightful comic send-up of the how-to essay. Nothing romantic about this. We've all had those jobs, and maybe we should follow Mary's lead and write about each of them.

One of my favorite books is *The Pillow Book of Sei Shonagon*, written over a thousand years ago by a lady-in-waiting to the Empress of Japan. Her usual strategy was to make lists: Things That Should Be Short; Things That Give a Clean Feeling; Adorable Things; Splendid Things, and so on. Her list of Things That

Should Be Large includes priests, fruit, houses, and the petals of yellow roses. Ray Bradbury made long lists of nouns as stimulation for stories. "These lists were the provocations, finally, that caused my better stuff to surface. I was feeling my way toward something honest, hidden under the trapdoor on the top of my skull." Bradbury would run through his list, pick a noun, begin writing, and in a page or two what he was calling a prose poem would turn into a story.

I have a Word folder of lists. I have lists of character names, first, sur-, and nick-; lists of titles, of ideas for stories, plays, poems, and screenplays; lists of quotes about writing and creativity; and lists of books I've read and want to read. I have a ninety-five-page single-spaced list of words I like and want to use in my stories. We all make lists, don't we? Of our top ten songs, our favorite movies, and so on. Christmas card lists, guest lists, birthday lists, to-do lists. And your characters make lists just like you do. Lists can be helpful for getting in touch with your usable past and with your obsessions. So let's try some list stories.

Fear and Loathing

Here's your title. "Why I'm Afraid of _____." Fill in the blank. It could be a proper name, but it doesn't need to be.

- Start each sentence of your story with "Because" and make a list of all the reasons for your fear.

- The story needs to be a hundred words long, let's say. The list should build, take us somewhere. It should not hit a single note, but modulate. Modulation is how you make music, not just rhythm. It should provide tension. You'll get it right in revision.

The Bag

A man is found dead in a flophouse. All of his belongings are in a green duffel bag. Open the bag and go through it.

- Make a list story about what you find. Be as precise as you can with each item.

- No need to comment—the accumulated items should add up to a portrait of the man (or woman, if you'd like).

Listserve

So here are some lists for you to make. Take five to ten minutes on each list initially. They will suggest events, emotions, people, you haven't considered in a while. What else do they suggest? Use the lists in the coming days and weeks for sources of material for your very short stories.

- List all the friends you've ever had but have lost contact with. Choose one of those friends, and write a story about what trouble came into his or her life.

- List all the moments you'd live over again for whatever reason. Pick one of those moments, one with trouble, one you'd like a do-over for, perhaps, and write that story in scene.

- List everything you've ever done that you are ashamed of. You know what to do!

All those stories came from lists we generated. Now let's borrow some lists. Shopping lists, to be precise. I pick up register tapes in the Publix parking lot and then try to imagine the lives of the people who did the shopping. But the Publix abbreviation system leaves a lot to be desired. What does "One Spec Care Wght" mean? Better to find the lists the customers brought with them. You'll find the lists in the plastic hand baskets or in the shopping carts. Better yet, you can go to grocerylists.org and read some of the thousands of shopping lists they have available.

Here's a pretty typical list. Tide seems to be the one indispensable item. The clothes are piling up in the hamper, I imagine. I'm

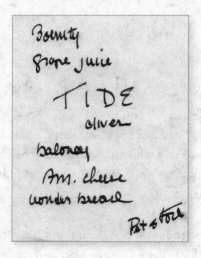

guessing the dirty dishes are piled in the sink. "Am. cheese" and "wonder bread" make me a little sad, maybe because they take me back to my own childhood. I hope, at least, they're going to make a grilled cheese sandwich. And who's going to eat the sandwich, and when? And I hope they're going to fry the "boloney." Delicious with eggs. And why the special trip to the pet store? Little Princess won't eat the house brand? The list is getting me thinking about a story or two. In one the pet store excursion is about buying a birthday gift for the little one, Ella, who's turning six. She wants a single African cichlid in a simple bowl because she read that there are eight hundred species of cichlids in Lake Malawi. She only wants one. Fish, not species. I'm thinking that she'll name it after a boy at school that she likes, and it will not live beyond the first week. But maybe I'll find out I'm wrong about that.

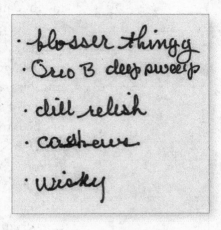

"Oreo B deep sweep"—we may have found the source of the dental problem. And he or she (the "wiskey" suggests a *he* to me) will need the floss picks after chewing the cashews—sans relish, we hope. No cookies tonight. I think he has a dentist's appointment tomorrow morning. And it's bothering him—he has a well-founded fear of dentists—a history of toothaches and botched fillings. He finishes the frozen fries, washes the supper dish and utensils, and sits in his recliner to watch the game. The "wiskey" is to help him relax. His dog Buster curls beside the chair and gobbles the cashews that drop to the floor. Our hero, call him Norman, plans on falling asleep in the La-Z-Boy and waking up just in time to shower, brush, and floss. The less time to think about drills, the better.

This next one's a shopping list, packing list, and a to-do list.

I imagine the first two items are "predator call" and "shotgun shells," but "clip-on dove"? And if he's going to take a knife, he'll need a sheath to hang it on. Coolers, of course, because nothing goes better with ammo and shotguns than beer. We might call our story "The Beer Hunter." And then on to the essentials. Having to remind himself to say so long to the wife is a classic. On the back of the list I found a phone number and Googled it, and it's the number of the Mountain View Motel in Killdeer, North Dakota. From the town's tourism website: "The Killdeer area is a hunter's paradise. Ring neck pheasants, sharp tail grouse, wild turkeys, elk, bighorn sheep, and whitetail or mule deer in the area." A bunch of buddies are off on their annual hunting trip. They've rented three or four rooms at the motel. In the past year, one of the guys got divorced, another lost his job, and one of our guys—the list writer—has learned a secret about one of the others. It's late. They're in one of the rooms pounding back beers after a fruitless day hunting. Our boy says something he maybe shouldn't have.

PRED CALL
SHOT SHELLS
CLIP-ON DOVE
VEST
WHISTLE
COOLERS
LICENSE
SHEATH
KNIFE
TOTE BAG
SAY BYE TO WIFE

To Market, to Market

Pick your list, imagine the list-maker, imagine the home, imagine what the items are for. Write. Get your own lists at the supermarket or online. Or try these:

After shave
rhubarb
sour cream

_____

condensed milk   Balmex rash cream
WIC Checks   depends?
Tinactin   Jolt cola
Prep H   lunchables

_____

mac & cheese
advil cool whip cheese whiz eggos
pop tarts birdseed
CAKE
chicken breast Fixodent Lean cuisines

~~1-800-685-43XX~~ (I learned that the crossed-out phone
number belonged to NCO Financial systems, called on one
Web page the country's "worst debt collection agency.")

_____

vitamin D   chick nuggits
Foljers   nutella
sardeans   mapel syrup
butt bath   supper glue

Once we pay attention, we notice that forms for our borrowing are all around us: want ads, the family Christmas letter, unsolicited e-mails about your lottery winnings, encyclopedia entries, job applications, résumés, blog posts, billboards, tweets, footnotes, assembly instructions, questionnaires, field notes, interviews, news reports, Facebook posts, travelogues, menus, car manuals, course syllabi, letters of complaint, book blurbs, letters of recommendation, weather reports, business cards, book reviews, movie reviews, taxonomies, horoscopes, movie pitches, police blotters, comic strips, confessions (forensic and liturgical), Post-it notes, wedding announcements, party invitations, FAQs, chat rooms, texts, list posts, rejection letters, magazine subscription cards, warning labels, lost dog posters, and so on.

A Word from Our Sponsor

A few moments ago, I saw a TV commercial for an erectile dysfunction medication and hurried here to the desk to write down the details of this domestic drama with a happy ending. Husband and wife are seeing their daughter off to college with what seems to be unwarranted delight. When daughter is gone, Mom and Dad snuggle happily and modestly on the couch in their clean, spacious, and well-lighted living room. Later they visit an art museum in their crisp summer outfits and insuppressible smiles and then a walk along a lakeshore. They conclude the day in two claw-foot bathtubs overlooking the sparkling waters of the lake at sunset or sunrise. Here's what I might do to tell their very short story. Give them names. Let Tom look at Alice, an arm's length away, up to her neck in soapy bubbles, and say . . . What? She replies, and the story begins. Use the name of the product for the title of your story.

Or maybe you want to use another commercial that has intrigued you. Watch a bunch of them on YouTube. They are almost all sixty seconds long. Just right for your One-Minute Fictions.

Formable

Or try some of these: write a very short story in the form of a business memo, but it can't be about business; in the form of a recipe, but it can't be about food; in the form of a prayer, but it can't be addressed to God; in the form of a *TV Guide* blurb, but it's not about a show.

Formless

About form, Donald Barthelme said, "Fragments are the only forms I trust." Fragments can suggest stories the way that archaeological artifacts do. Most of the fragments I collect in my notebook are snippets of conversations overheard that might communicate, as Henry James said, "the virus of suggestion." Here are a few.

- "I can do everything with this phone."

  "Can you send a fax?"

  "Not *every* everything."

- "Bobby doesn't believe in climate change, but he does believe in zombies."
- "I accidentally watched the news today."
- "He's always one letter behind when he dances to 'YMCA.'"
- "I'd like my steak tartare well done."

Keep your notebook with you and your ears wide open.

The Art of the Glimpse

My task, which I am trying to achieve is, by the power of the written word, to make you hear, to make you feel—it is, before all, to make you see.

—JOSEPH CONRAD

LET'S LOOK at some visual images in this chapter and try to develop stories from them. We'll start with a photograph. I love photography and especially love snapshots of people being themselves. These shots offer the viewer character, setting, mood, tone, mystery, event, and may even suggest plot. What more could a writer ask for? Here's a photo from my own collection of snapshots.

———

Use this photo or get one of your own. Perhaps you have a favorite photographer. Search for her photos online. Or go through the family album or your Shutterfly file or wherever your images are stored. And do the following.

Every Picture Tells a Story

Study your chosen photograph for a few minutes. Look at it closely. Note the composition, the light and shadow, the expression, the subjects' hands, and so on. Now give the photograph a title. Even if it has one, give it your own. Okay, now what does the title suggest? Do you detect thematic material already? Write about the title for a few minutes.

Look at the photo again. It will suggest a mood or perhaps an emotion. This might be, in fact, what originally attracted you to the photograph. Write down the mood on a blank sheet of paper and freewrite on that mood. (That is, write without thinking or stopping for five minutes, let's say. Use your stopwatch because you don't want your eyes leaving the paper.) Forget the photo while you're doing this. The emotion or mood is important. Don't let yourself brood over it, write as quickly as you can.

Back to the picture. Where are we? And when, what year? What season? What time of day? Write about this place and this time. Give the place a name and a population. Take a walk down the main street. Look at the buildings and the businesses there, the folks out on the sidewalks. Write about this place.

Look at the photograph again and decide whose story you want to tell. Give this person a name and an address in this town.

So now we have a central character with a name and a place with a name. We have a title, a mood, a setting. Let's consider plot. This central character must want something. What is that? Why does she want it? The motivation should be intense. There must be something at stake. Who or what is in conflict with the central character? In other words, what are the obstacles in the central character's way? What will prevent her from getting what she wants? How will she struggle? Will she get what she wants? What are the moments of complication? Climax? Think and write.

Now select a point of view from which to tell the story. Have the point-of-view character or the narrator make a statement about the central character, telling you something you don't already know. Ask the questions suggested by the statement. Answer them. Write some more. We're just collecting information and getting ready to write.

All of these questions of plot, character, point of view, do not have to be answered immediately. In fact, you probably want to avoid thinking overmuch about what happens in the story just yet.

> **Photography is a reality so subtle that it becomes more real than reality.**
>
> —*Alfred Stieglitz*

You don't want to tie your characters into behavior that is something you want and might not be what they want. The point is that now you have a lot of raw material with which to begin the construction of your story. And all in a very short time.

Now try this. Think about the photographer. Who took this picture? What was in his mind as he looked through the viewfinder? What happened just before he took the picture? What or who is just outside the frame? What happened just after the photo was taken? Did the photographer and the subject speak? About what?

This exercise is easier to do if you have people in the photograph, as I said, but it works as well with photos in which the absence of people is palpable. Consider this photo by Don Bullens.

A Thousand Words

Every abandoned home or business represents a failed dream. Here's a photo of a defunct bar and restaurant on Grassy Key, Florida, a place where locals and tourists once gathered to break bread, tell stories, sing karaoke on Wednesday nights, and cele-brate the good life. Just another day in paradise, as they say. What went wrong? Who is Jo-Jo? Anthony Trollope once said of writing stories that it was a "hard, grinding industry." The same could be said for a running a restaurant. What do you do when you've devoted thirty years of your life, your blood, sweat, and tears, into an enterprise that goes under despite your best efforts? And what remains? A fading sign, an empty chair, a car's bucket seat, a pointless mailbox, the ragged grass repossessing the pavement, the extrinsic palms, and the unforgiving sun. Imagine the closing day. Imagine the owner looking one last time at the silent place he has not been able to salvage or sell. Imagine his thoughts and feelings. Imagine him walking away from his dream, his paradise lost. Write about those few minutes. Do it in a thousand words—that's what a picture's worth.

Any derelict or deserted home or business will engage your sense of wonder. What happened here? Who were the people that gave it life and where did they go? Now let's try another photo. Don Bullens again.

Some details to consider: that bank of eleven newspaper vending machines, the thirteen gingerbread men on the wall, the twenty-five carved pineapples on the eaves, the three fallen traffic posts, the nine scruffy plants, and the single empty planter.

I collect old postcards, like I collect every kind of ephemera, because only what is temporary is of lasting value. People use postcards—or did—to communicate with specific people, family and friends. People who travel believe in what St. Augustine said: "The world is a book and he who doesn't travel only reads one page."

And speaking of travel, when we travel, visit new places, we tend to be alert, to notice things that we might not ordinarily pay attention to. We notice the unusual flora and fauna, the peculiar architectural details, the illuminating local customs, the strange food, the exotic aromas. Travel trains us to notice. We are open to new experiences; we welcome new interaction with people. We are assertively curious. Everything we see attracts our attention. We are, in fact, a lot like fiction writers when we are travelers. And that's a state we want to try to foster in our daily lives. To be travelers when we're at home. At least when we're at the writing desk.

Why do we travel? As Mark Twain said, "Travel is fatal to prejudice, bigotry, and narrow-mindedness, and many of our people need it sorely on these accounts. Broad, wholesome, charitable views of men and things cannot be acquired by vegetating in one little corner of the earth all one's lifetime." Here are two postcards, one vintage, one contemporary:

Maranacook Lodge within 50 feet of Lake Maranacook, Me.   B- / 0 / 4

Hotel Constantinupolis, Corfu

Wish You Were Here

Use one of these cards and write a very short story about the place and the people you imagine there. Maybe do a little research on the place. Invent the person who is writing the card. She needs a name. Traveling alone or with friends or family? Tell the story in the small space you have on the reverse side of the postcard. You only have half of the card. Write small. The other half is reserved for address and stamp, of course. So address it to someone. The person addressed is the sender's only reader. What does she want that person to know? Not to know? Study the photo, let the place and the atmosphere carry you away. Set the mood. Use evocative details. Not all vacations are happy ones.

The paintings of Edward Hopper have inspired Joyce Carol Oates to write interior monologues for the characters in her poem "Edward Hopper's Nighthawks, 1942." They also inspired Tom Waits to write *Nighthawks at the Diner* and Canadian indie rock band the Weakerthans to write two songs. Hopper's *Room in New York* inspired Michèle-Jessica Fièvre's very short story. Find the painting here in full color: http://www.edwardhopper.net/room-in-new-york.jsp.

ROOM IN NEW YORK

Greg didn't look up from the paper, and his voice was unreadable. "They're saying you killed Joe, Madeleine. Why in the world would they be saying that?"

She didn't answer at first; her index finger kept on playing *La Bohème* on the piano. Finally, she spoke up, her voice sandpaper rough. "Joe is dead, Greg. And I'm missing. What else would the paper say?"

She raised her fingers to her throat and closed them around the locket as if she only now remembered that it contained an old photograph of Joe. She unclasped the locket, took off her wedding ring, and slipped the jewelry in her pocket.

Greg's voice didn't falter. "Did you kill him? Tell me, Madeleine—when you came here last night, was he already dead?"

Her expression stayed flat and blank; her index finger kept on moving. "Do you want me to leave?" she asked, glancing at the X-Acto knife on the table, and then at Greg's pale arm, thinking how easily she might cut the soft skin.

Greg nodded one of his slow, knowing nods, ran his hand through his hair, smoothing it down. "Part of me does."

Madeleine frowned. She pictured the bright stripe of blood, Greg's shock and pain. She played with these thoughts for several moments before turning toward him. "Joe never stopped you from seeing me before."

Greg put down the newspaper and, as he rose from the couch, a hot breeze blew through the window.

We peer through an open window at an unreadable man reading the newspaper and a composed young woman playing the piano. Secrets, lies, and betrayal all at work in this subdued tableau. Violence, real and imagined, and operatic music.

Exteriors

An ekphrastic poem or story is a description of a work of visual art. Let a work of art be your subject and your inspiration. You're looking for a story, as Michèle did, for trouble, for a central char-

> **Writing is the painting of the voice.**
>
> —*Voltaire*

acter. On the next page you'll see a copy of a lithograph by Edvard Munch that you are no doubt familiar with, *The Scream*. Let it carry you away. Study it. Make notes. In his novel *Do Androids Dream of Electric Sheep?*, Philip K. Dick's hero encounters *The Scream*, which is described like this: "The painting showed a hair-less, oppressed creature with a head like an inverted pear, its hands clapped in horror to its ears, its mouth open in a vast soundless scream. Twisted ripples of the creature's torment, echoes of its cry, flooded out into the air surrounding it: the man or woman, which-ever it was, had become contained by its own howl." Who are those two figures behind our screamer and what are they up to? The ships on the fjord are arriving or leaving? From or to where? Is that a church spire or town hall in the distance?

Interiors

And here is an etching by Edward Hopper, *East Side Interior*. A woman at a sewing machine surrounded by comforts of home: the rocker, the lamp, the framed artwork, the hanging plant. But she's staring out the opened window into the bright light of all that is not home and comfort. What is her name? What is the trouble in her life? What does she want and what is stopping her from getting it?

Adspeak

Let's consider for a moment the graphic novel, a narrative form that uses sequential artwork to help tell the story. The form evolved, some would say, from comics like *Superman*. The first mass market graphic novel was *The Silver Surfer* by Stan Lee and

Jack Kirby. And now we have *The Watchmen* series, Neil Gaiman's *The Sandman*, and Art Spiegelman's graphic novel of the Holocaust, *Maus*. We're not writing novels, however, we're writing flash. So let's try out graphic short-short stories by using, at first, the art that we find around us in the world. Ads. The idea is to take an illustrated ad, like this one for Lysol Disinfectant from the mid-thirties, which you can find at this website: https://commons .wikimedia.org/wiki/File:The_poise_that_knowledge_gives.jp. Print out the ad, cut out the copy, use the artwork, write your story, and glue the story onto the space where the original copy had been.

So now it's your turn to write a graphic short-short story. The story can be inspired by anything about the artwork that captures your imagination. It does not have to be about the product. Who are these people in the ads? Where do they live? What are their fears? You have your title in the Lysol ad, "The Poise That Knowledge Gives," and perhaps even your theme. You've got a central character. Give her a name and an address. She's described as being fastidiously well-groomed and sure of herself in every detail. That's the self she presents to the public. But what about her private self? You've got a lamp casting a strange light on the back wall. Where is she? What year is this? Who is she staring at? Is she about to speak? Is she about to listen? She seems dressed for a night out in that satin evening dress. Where is she going and with whom, if anyone? What is she feeling right now? What is she thinking? Maybe she's thinking about what's missing in her life or about what keeps her up at night. What does she want? What's stopping her from getting it? How will she struggle? And that obscured painting on the wall behind her. What is it a picture of and how does that inform your story?

Those of us of a certain age will remember the World's Most Perfectly Developed Man, Charles Atlas, famous for coming to the rescue of skinny guys having beach sand kicked in their faces by obnoxious, hormone-enhanced bullies. Atlas was one of many body builders looking to turn America's ninety-seven-pound weaklings into he-men in a series of mail-order ads in comic books—staples of the muscle industry. Joe Weider promised to add three inches of steel-like muscle to your biceps in just three days. Ben Rebhuhn would show you how to develop "spaceman strength and endurance" and how to be "astronaut-tough" while gaining up to fifty pounds of "mighty muscles." (All this before the obesity epidemic.) Knowing their audience, the body-building ads often graphically mimicked the comic books they were in. George F. Jowett ran something called the Body Sculpture Club, and one of his comic strip ads was titled "He was a 'SHRIMP!' to the boys in the baths!" (Hmm, with that title one might go in any number of directions.) In the eight narrative panels that followed, our unlikely hero, Shrimp, goes from wearing water wings in the swimming pool and being shunned and heckled by the merciless mesomorphs flexing their adolescent muscles at poolside, to—in a daring bit of metafiction— reading a Jowett ad in a comic book, perhaps this very comic book, and signing up for the training program, to winning both the Best Swimmer and the All-Around Athlete of the Year awards at the annual banquet. "And he deserves it," a member of the audience says. You can find the graphic short-short story here: https://www.pinterest.com/pin/525865693959775140/.

With the "Shrimp" strip, you have a central character and you have themes of ridicule, self-esteem, bullies, hope . . . what else? You'll tell your very short story by replacing the text in the thought and speech balloons and in the description boxes with your own. You'll use the obligatory coupon space and the text space below the strip to enhance the narrative in surprising ways.

Don't restrict yourself to comic strip ads. Any graphic ad with text will do. Ads for X-ray specs, hypno-coins, ant farms, darling pet monkeys that fit in the palm of your hand, sea monkeys, Rosicrucians, ads for health and hygiene products, home appliances, automobiles, ads that promise to end baldness, and ads that promise pain eradication.

And now you can try your hand at graphic micro-fiction:

EXPLODING CIGAR

An imitation Cigar that fills with tobacco. When half smoked, explodes and shoots the tobacco out. Can be filled again as often as you wish. Perfectly harmless. **Sample cigar with 10 exploding pellets by mail for........ 10c**

ROYAL NOVELTY CO., 250 East Ave., SOUTH NORWALK, CT.

Perhaps you'd prefer to do your own graphics. There are several comic websites that will help you frame your graphic story. Some even come with characters drawn for you. Your graphics don't have to be elaborate, just articulate. Stick people can work. I met an undergraduate student some years ago who asked me if he could write and submit graphic short stories, and I surprised myself by saying yes. I'd already read his short prose—some of it about comic-book-obsessed teenage boys—and was much impressed and entertained. In one of those conventional stories I learned that all comic book stores get their new stock on Wednesdays,

I started drawing at a very young age. Writing a story wasn't satisfying, but to actually draw our own world—it's like controlling your own dreams.

—*Daniel Clowes*

and on Wednesdays you could find Jarod Roselló's characters and Jarod himself at a comic book store somewhere in Miami. Jarod's now teaching graphic fiction in the MFA program at University of South Florida in Tampa. And here's one of his graphic stories.

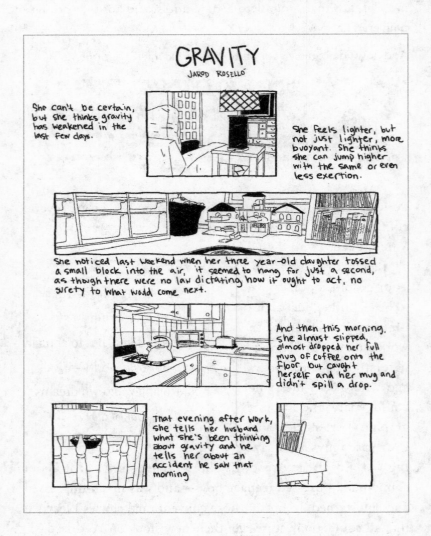

a small SUV flipped on its side, windshield cracked, the frame crumpled, airbags deployed, a car seat lying face down in the road a few feet away, and a man in blue jeans and a faded red t-shirt sitting on the curb with his face in his hands.

He tells her that he wanted to stop the car and get out, to offer assistance if he could, aid if possible, but instead he accelerated and went to work, and he would like to know what she makes of that.

She takes her glass of water, holds it in the air, then releases it. He gestures to catch it, but it doesn't fall, it only floats in the air, suspended in the space between them.

And then she stands and tells him what she's been meaning to tell him.

Gravity, the natural force that tends to cause physical things to move toward each other, is decidedly out of whack in our story where husband and wife are moving away from each other and a coffee mug hovers in midair. The noun *gravity* refers to a serious situation or problem, and we certainly do have grave trouble in this very brief graphic story (273 words and 10 illustrations). The brilliance of the story lies partially in the "certain strangeness" of the capricious gravity, and otherwise in the contrast between the geometric restraint of the illustrations and the narrative chaos expressed by the unembellished prose, all of which move the story forward and build tension in a way that reminds me of the filmmaker Sergei Eisenstein's theory of montage, meaning the unity of shots of seemingly unrelated objects in the same film sequence so that they take on a new relationship to each other in the viewer's mind. On-screen, you see a child asleep in her bed, a plush bunny tucked under her arm, as a soft breeze ruffles the linen curtains, but you hear the thumps of approaching footsteps and then silence and then the creak of an opening door, and you watch the child stir in her sleep, and you hear the snick of the latch bolt into the strike plate and see a shadow cover the child's face like a shroud. The whole of the visual and aural images is greater than the sum of its parts. At the movies and in Jarod's story. And note the illustrations: an empty living room; the child's room, neat as a pin; the cozy, spotless kitchen; the unset dining table, and the unoccupied chairs. And outside: an unpeopled landscape with lamppost; a stockade fence and a cloud of trees; a final portrait of a tidy house in a leafy, unpeopled neighborhood. Jarod's graphics never show us what we're being told in the prose. What would be the point?

> Art begins the moment the creaking of a boot on the soundtrack occurs against a different visual shot and thus gives rise to corresponding associations.
>
> —*Sergei Eisenstein*

Here's another very short graphic story by Jarod told from the point of view of a reminiscent first-person narrator, featuring wide-eyed children and inscrutable cats.

WE ARE SAFE

by JAROD ROSELLÓ

WHEN THEY STARTED YELLING

WE TOOK THE CATS AND PUT THEM IN OUR ROOM.

WE THOUGHT WE WERE SAVING THEM.

THE CATS WERE BETTER AT HIDING THAN WE WERE.

WE WERE TOO LARGE TO HIDE WELL.

WE DID WHAT WE COULD. WE LAY IN OUR BEDS WITH THE BLANKETS UP OVER OUR HEADS, PRETENDING TO BE ASLEEP, HOPING SLEEP WOULD SAVE US.

SOME NIGHTS NEITHER OF US COULD SLEEP

WE LAY PERFECTLY STILL, STARING AT THE CEILING

I USED TO HANG MY ARM OVER THE SIDE OF THE BED

WAITING FOR OUR CATS TO COME TO ME.

TO RUB THEIR BODIES AGAINST MY HAND

I ALWAYS FELL ASLEEP BEFORE THEY CAME

———

Here the illustrations depict the younger brother's memories and dreams, and those expressive eyes let us in on the boys' emotions: fear, confusion, exuberance, and relief. Contrast those eyes to the blank eyes of the dream cats. And note the conspicuous absence of those who must be hidden from.

Shorts Illustrated

And now it's your turn. A very short story that you write and illustrate. The illustrations can be simple, of course, simple and eloquent. If you think you can't draw, remember the words of Vincent van Gogh: "If you hear a voice within you say 'you cannot paint,' then by all means paint, and that voice will be silenced," and by all means draw. Or borrow. Outsider artist Henry Darger, who wrote and illustrated a fifteen-thousand-page, single-spaced manuscript called *The Story of the Vivian Girls, in What Is Known as the Realms of the Unreal, of the Glandeco-Angelinian War Storm, Caused by the Child Slave Rebellion,* appropriated his images from newspapers, comic books, magazines, and especially coloring books. He cut out the images he wanted, enlarged them, and then traced the images, using wax paper, onto his paper. Try that. Or try the simple websites that offer comic templates and even characters. Or you can take one of your very short stories and add the illustrations. You need characters, plot, and images, and all are important.

Long and Short

Thought is only a flash between two long nights, but the flash is everything.

—Henri Poincaré

Let's try writing some flash sequences, very short stories that are connected in the way of a story cycle, as described in *The Composite Novel: The Short Story Cycle in Transition* by Ann Morris and Maggie Dunn: "Literary work composed of shorter texts that though individually complete and autonomous are interrelated in a coherent whole according to one or more organizing principles." Those principles often are related to theme, setting, event, and/or character. Let's begin with a tetralogy, which is any series of four related dramatic or literary compositions. Shakespeare wrote two tetralogies in his history plays: *Richard II, Henry IV* (1 and 2), and *Henry V*; and *Henry VI* (1, 2 and 3) and *Richard III*. The tetralogy has its roots in Greek theater, where playwrights wrote three tragedies and a satire in competition. Lawrence Durrell wrote *The Alexandria Quartet* consisting of four novels. John Updike's four Rabbit books form a tetralogy. Now you get to write your short-short tetralogy. But first a bit about haiku and about Northrop Frye.

The haiku follows several conventions. The traditional haiku consists of three lines. The first and third lines contain five syllables, the second, seven. The traditional subject matter is a description of a location, of natural phenomena, like flowers, snow, or frogs, or of an everyday occurrence. The imagery presents a meditative snapshot of the universe, as it were, an intensive moment of perception, favoring a flash of intuitive insight over logic and thought. The haiku seeks to capture the qualities of experiencing the natural world uncluttered by "ideas." Or as William Carlos Williams had it: "No ideas but in things." It presents a clear picture via concrete imagery in the manner of the objective correlative mentioned earlier, so as to arouse the emotions and suggest, perhaps, spiritual insight. The haiku is usually set during a particular season or month, which helps to establish the tone or the mood of the piece. The poet describes her subject in an exceptional and unexpected way without explicit commentary or judgment. Simplicity is more valued than cleverness. No showing off. Here's how the Haiku Society of America defines haiku: *A haiku is a short poem that uses imagistic language to convey the essence of an experience of nature or the season intuitively linked to the human condition.* Haiku means "beginning verse" in Japanese. The reader goes on when the poem is finished in the imagistic and emotional directions suggested by the poem.

Here's a haiku by Matsuo Bashō, translated by William George Aston:

> *On a withered branch*
> *A crow is sitting*
> *This autumn eve.*

The syllabic count did not survive the translation, you'll note. We'll come back to haiku in a moment. But now let's consider Northrop Frye's theory of literary archetypes. We don't need to go deep here, since we're only using the archetypes as a guide in writing our tetralogy.

DAILY / SEASONAL / HUMAN CYCLE	MYTH (BASED UPON AN ARCHETYPAL PATTERN OF HUMAN EXPERIENCE)	LITERARY GENRE
dawn / *spring* / birth	the birth, revival, resurrection of the hero	comedy; pastoral; idyll
zenith / *summer* / marriage or triumph	the triumph, marriage, or apotheosis of the hero	romance
sunset / *autumn* / impending death	the fall, sacrifice, isolation, or death of the hero	tragedy; elegy
night / *winter* / dissolution	the unheroic nature of the hero	irony; satire

A Year in the Life

Here's the exercise. Your haiku-inspired stories will be three hundred words or fewer. One page, in other words. The stories will be linked by character, by place, by theme, by subject matter. Call it "The Four Seasons," if you like—four seasons in a character's life. Maybe listen to Vivaldi while you're writing. The stories should stand alone and also function as a whole—the whole being greater than the sum of the parts. And the seasons and moods correspond to Frye's theory of archetypes. You can start with any season. Follow Frye's patterns, but feel free to also follow the accidents. Let spring reflect revival in a comic or idyllic way, and so forth through the year.

Here's a very short tetralogy by Robert Busby.

SEASONUS EXODUS

FEBRUARY

Power and telephone lines hang limp from utility poles. From the window the old wife can see for hundreds of yards through a clear-cut emptiness where before much couldn't be seen past twenty feet. In the wake of the storm, oaks and cedars lie uprooted or snapped in half or, in the case of the young pines and firs, doubled over completely, held to the earth like ready catapults by the twelve-hour strain of ice settled in their branches.

Their first year of retirement, she and her husband had taken a charter bus tour through the Northeast and found themselves stranded and forced to hole up in a Days Inn to wait out a late autumn snowstorm and a ten-below wind-chill just outside Freeport, Maine. That brutal cold had produced something tranquil and beautiful in their motel window. But this one that snuck across the Mid-South last night, she thinks, looks more like some tornado had blown through than any ice storm. Like cancer in marrow had escaped bone.

APRIL

Condensation veils the windows like partial glaucoma. The white blanket of a strange, early spring frost draws back now into the shadow of the forest, persuaded there by the sunlight crawling across the backyard and glistening the length of wet blades of grass. The ground looks like a candy wrapper.

"What about the car again?" her husband says, his hand on the handle of the sliding patio door.

"I said," the wife calls from their bedroom, "don't forget your cardigan. There was a frost late last night."

Her husband nods at the vines, their fruit rock-solid and crying dew in the midmorning light. Finds himself dreaming of fresh tomato sandwiches, lunch on the beach.

AUGUST

A storm brews off the Gulf Coast. A gull beak-shovels guts from a dead seal half submerged in the warm sand. Purple flesh clings to the bird's lower jaw. The couple make dinner plans the clouds threaten to postpone.

"I hear Harborside Landing's good," the old wife says. The gull knocks back more carrion. She brushes sand from the swatch of half-calf below her Capris.

"Is it safe to eat there?" her husband asks.

She shrugs. "It's on the bay. Where better to get seafood than by the water?"

A wave thrusts towards the shore like a clenched fist and the froth unfolds before the couple. Suddenly young, the wife dips a toe in the tide and laughs, rubs her wet, bare foot on her husband's calf. Water maps a trail down his sandy varicose vein. He holds her wrist in silence, the two of them frozen beneath a gray sky like Pompeii lovers.

He says, "I just don't know about eating at a place called Herbicide."

OCTOBER

The wind shifts oak leaves towards the heavens, braids them into some combusted cyclone that sends a squirrel bobbing like a cork back to its winter stash, acornless. The widower watches from a chair at the table in the breakfast nook, across from where she would have sat. Legs crossed, his argyle socks interrupt khaki hem and Rockports. The brief solitude that he had sometimes sought, that his trouble hearing would allow, now crowds the house. The squirrel returns to the acorn it has dropped, massages it back into the cavity of its jaw, and returns to its stash beneath the tree still doubled over like a winded runner from last winter's storm. Providing, the man thinks. But who does he provide for now? Who provides for him?

He drops his hand on the table, palm flat, a prelude to motion. The leaves do not rake themselves. Get your cardigan, he tells himself in her way. And then the rake.

We begin with devastation and proceed through a series of subtle, comic, but alarming physical insults, get a moment's reprieve before the isolation, the grief, the silence, the sadness, the widower's small triumph, keeping his wife's memory alive with a sweater. He and the trees have survived.

Seven Deadly Sins

Lust, gluttony, greed, sloth, wrath, envy, and pride. You know them; you've committed them. Now you can write a very short story cycle about them. You might want to begin your stories with epigraphs from the Bible and let the epigraph guide the narratives:

1. Lust: "But I tell you that anyone who looks at a woman lustfully has already committed adultery with her in his heart." (Matthew 5:28)

2. Gluttony: "For drunkards and gluttons become poor, and drowsiness clothes them in rags." (Proverbs 23:21)

3. Greed: "Having lost all sensitivity, they have given themselves over to sensuality so as to indulge in every kind of impurity, with a continual lust for more." (Ephesians 4:19)

4. Sloth: "The way of the sluggard is blocked with thorns, but the path of the upright is a highway." (Proverbs 15:19)

5. Wrath: "A gentle answer turns away wrath, but a harsh word stirs up anger." (Proverbs 15:1)

6. Envy: "Therefore, rid yourselves of all malice and all deceit, hypocrisy, envy, and slander of every kind. Like newborn babies, crave pure spiritual milk, so that by it you may grow up in your salvation." (1 Peter 2:1–2)

7. Pride: "Pride goes before destruction, a haughty spirit before a fall." (Proverbs 16:18)

Here's a very short story from the Bible illustrating wrath.

THE MASSACRE OF THE INNOCENTS

When Herod realized that he had been outwitted by the Magi, he was furious, and he gave orders to kill all the boys in Bethlehem and its vicinity who were two years old and under, in accordance with the time he had learned from the Magi. Then what was said through the prophet Jeremiah was fulfilled: "A voice is heard in Ramah, weeping and great mourning, Rachel weeping for her children and refusing to be comforted, because they are no more."

And here's a short-short story by Leslie Taylor illustrating greed, among other sins.

SUPPER CLUB BLACKMAIL

Jillian's brother's gold cuff links clinked against the empty wineglass as he shoveled more rare meat into his churning mouth. They sat across from each other, here, in the oldest ol' supper club in Salina, Kansas, a town two generations past sunset. Her brother wanted to bring them here to gloat, but he had portrayed it as magnanimous. Both were overdressed, and the waiter had assumed they were a couple celebrating. No, she informed him, mourning. She rotated the glass of water with her fingertips, eyeing a smudge of lipstick, which she only wore when the world expected. The father's lawyer, a young man from Harvard, was having dinner there too. He was sitting by himself in a booth across the room, his back to them, the glow of his smartphone keeping him company.

Jillian's brother said, between bites of prime rib and the machine grinding of teeth, that Pop's inheritance worked out for the best. "Or maybe the old man wanted to give you an excuse to finally find a man. Maybe grow your hair out, look pretty like you do now." Jillian knew her interest in women was the reason for their father's hateful eyes and malicious will. Her brother was the proud papa's boy; a good ol' boy businessman, like "Pop." She barely spoke, let her brother chew out insults between the meat, and imagined shoving her glass into his face.

Jillian's brother got up to use the restroom. His tree trunk, linebacker body physically intimidated most, but it hadn't gotten him a wife. After he left, his cell phone buzzed; he had left it next to the plate of oozing red meat. Jillian knew the unlock code (his birthday), could read upside down (a useful trick in a family like this), and had no problem spying on the bastard (she never did). The message read, "Hey baby." She responded, typing upside down, "I miss you." The phone quietly shook. "I'm right here." Her neck went taut like a rope. Out of the corner of her eye she could see the young lawyer, handsome, effeminate, texting rapidly in the soft light of his phone. Another message. "I can't wait to have you for dessert."

Jillian's brother sat back down. He picked up the fork and knife then dropped them. His phone was gone. He asked where it was, she showed him. She was excited to tell him her terms for the inheritance or tell the world about what he did in his closet. They understood each other for the first time. Her salvation had arrived.

The story of a family that has forsaken love, honesty, and compassion for greed, stealth, and manipulation. A family worthy of a Greek tragedy, artfully dissected in a single scene. In the end, the worm turns, and a charade is unmasked.

Consider also writing a story cycle based on the Ten Commandments, on the Corporal Works of Mercy, on the Ten Plagues, and on the Seven Principal Virtues. You can be funny and ironic, of course.

Eyewitness

Akira Kurosawa's 1950 movie *Rashomon* was based on Ryūnosuke Akutagawa's short story "In a Grove." The term *Rashomon effect* refers to the self-serving and contradictory interpretations of the same event by different people. In this case the story of theft, murder, and rape. Same story. Four ways. The Russians have a saying, or so I've read, "Nobody lies like an eyewitness." Create a situation. A crime will work well. Or an accident. Something dramatic. Now let the four or five people involved tell their versions of the incident.

In the Worst Way

Stories are about trouble. Everything that you don't want to happen to yourself or your family or your friends *should* happen to your characters. Chekhov said we should write about what keeps us up at night. With that thought in mind, I made a list of what I think are the worst things that can happen in a person's life. Read my list. Write your own. Here's mine (I'll keep it to ten): death of a child; death of a spouse; death of a parent; sick child; jail; poverty/homelessness; addiction; mental illness/Alzheimer's; physical illness/chronic pain; betrayal. The Holmes-Rahe Life Stress Inventory lists forty-three harrowing events that can lead to the breakdown in your health, from the death of a spouse, divorce, and separation to, not surprisingly, Christmas and minor violations of the law. Make your list; write a very short story about each event. Get specific. What kind of betrayal? What kind of addiction? Or go to the Holmes-Rahe list online and write forty-three short-short stories.

A Month of Stories

Write a very short story every day for a month. If there are holidays during your chosen month, write the story about the holiday. And there are holidays every month. If you decide to write your thirty stories during June, you'd have Flag Day, Father's Day, Juneteenth, and perhaps some local observances. Otherwise, try this plan.

- Week 1: stories about family
- Week 2: stories about work
- Week 3: stories about love
- Week 4: stories about death and dying
- Days 29–31: stories about childhood

Seven Dwarfs

The dwarfs who took in Snow White after she fled from her wicked stepmother were not named in the Grimm Brothers telling of the folk tale. They got their familiar names in a 1937 Disney movie. Doc, Dopey, Bashful, Grumpy, Sneezy, Sleepy, and Happy. Six adjectives and a job title. The allegorical names for the seven miners seem a little dismissive and restrictive, making them what E. M. Forster called flat characters. Your job is to give them each some depth, nuance, and a voice. Let each of the dwarfs tell his story in turn, and in his story reveal a secret and express emotions previously unspoken.

Home for the Holidays

It's always a good idea in fiction to get families together at ritual events, at weddings, funerals, baptisms, reunions, and holidays. There's bound to be trouble. And that's what you're looking for. So follow a family through the year and write about their gatherings in a series of very short stories: New Year's, Easter or Passover, Independence Day, Labor Day, family reunion, a wedding, Thanksgiving Day, and Christmas. Anyone die during the year? Marry? Divorce? Have a baby? Anyone arrested?

The Way of All Flash

*Thinking up stories is hard. Getting them to come to you
is easier.*

—Lynda Barry

Konstantin Stanislavski wrote that feelings can't be commanded; they can only be coaxed. We might say the same
for stories. We can't make them appear, but we can summon
them, entice them by applying the restrictions of writing exercises. Just a reminder from Willa Cather about this writing business: "There is no such thing as freedom in art. The first thing an
artist does when he begins a new work is to lay down the barriers
and limitations." Let's write:

A Red Flash

Let's begin with fairy tales, which for many of us were our introduction to literature. In fairy tales, we first learned what it was like
to be a human being. We learned about trouble and struggle and
triumph and tension and suspense. And we learned how to tell sto-

ries by listening to them, in the way that we learned the alphabet by singing it. Retelling fairy tales for YA readers has become a cottage industry for fantasy writers. Neil Gaiman retells a Snow White/Sleeping Beauty composite tale in *The Sleeper and the Spindle*. But one might choose realism over fantasy with marvelous results. Your job in this exercise is to transform a traditional fairy tale—perhaps your favorite—into a contemporary tale. Here's Lynne Barrett's very short retelling of "Little Red Riding Hood."

LITTLE RED RETURNS

These days you are a strawberry blonde. Back in town after a long rest at a woodland spa, peace, yoga, massages, excellent sleep in a rustic cottage, you feel ready. Tonight you're with a backwoodsman you picked up out there, young, stalwart, unblemished. You take him clubbing, enjoying his astonishment as you go from one dizzy crowd to the next.

Wouldn't you know it, you run into Vülf, entering Fungi as you leave.

"Where are you going, my dear?" His deep voice catches you, the same growl that, intoning on records, drew all the little girls, including you, back when.

"Oh, you know," you tell him, "we have to take it all in. We're headed to Anni's party at Rose Red, later on."

"Ah, Anni's party. I'll be there," he says, "my dear." His rasp raises the hair on your neck.

You want the old Vülf to swallow you and you know it. You've been in that darkness before. When you were with him his world surrounded you. You traveled with his pack and wore clothes he designed, the chic of the hood. You shared his nightly wandering, lived on his diet of steak and

Veuve Clicquot and coca, went back to his lair and, while his music pounded around you, shook to his snarls. You cried, didn't you, when he threw you away? You've dreamed of him, haven't you: tall, charcoal, and silver.

At Anni's party, he's not there. Anni herself has made more than one comeback, and the white streak in her black hair seems now to be the only natural thing about her. You've heard the young models call her Granny, but still she reigns. The club is a hall of flattering pink mirrors. At one end, the bar glows, its long curve of rose-etched glass lit from within. You dance with your woodsman, turning and turning till you catch a glimpse of Vülf.

He beckons and you go to his red velvet corner. He offers you your choice, but you take the same mineral water that he's having.

He pours it and grins. His smile is dark.

"Why, Vülf, what happened to that big tooth you had?"

"Ah, the diamond fang. You remember that, sweetheart? I cashed it in. You heard I had a patch of trouble, no doubt."

"I heard something about those arms you had."

"The his and hers Uzis under the back seat? They were quite legal, I had the papers, but certain parties were looking for an excuse to take me down. Fortunately, a whisper reached me."

"I know what sharp ears you had."

"They thought they'd snare me on a weapons count. They impounded everything they could get their hands on, but in the end found nothing to charge me with, my dear. I had to sell a few little items," that dark grin again, "but I'm safe."

"Are you sure? Once they go after you—"

"Why? What have you heard?" His long face looks at you slyly, warily.

"Not a thing. So you're back in business?"

"Oh yes, I'm cooking up a sweet production deal. My strength, you know, has always been sensing what new wildness kids have in them."

"Everyone knows what an eye you have for talent."

"That's right. Indeed, I'm on the prowl tonight to see what I can find. So happy to come upon *you*, my dear. I think perhaps it's you I overlooked before."

But you know better. You have no talent. And if he's considering you, looking at you fondly—fondly!—patting your hand, well, he's no good to you anymore.

You smile and squeeze his hairy wrist and go find your woodsman on the dance floor, surrounded by famished beauties. You carry him off, out into the early morning starlight. You run your hand along his strong young arm. While you still can, you howl.

———

The beloved fairy tale turned on its head, told in second-person point of view and not the traditional third. Part of the fun of this short-short story is its reliance on our knowledge of the ur-story and our complicity in the unfolding plot. Here the fake has become natural, prey has become predator, and rescuer, the prey.

Newsflash

Some stories are ripped from the headlines. The newspaper is a great source of material for fiction. I've gotten the germ for many stories that way. What the news stories offer is a climactic event. And your job is to imagine what led up to that event. Or to imagine the aftermath. And here are a few actual headlines you might want to play with:

- Grits Argument Turns Violent
- A Game with Handcuffs, Blindfold and a Paring Knife
- Man Wearing Chicken Suit Robs Kroger
- Homeless Man Under House Arrest
- The Liar, the Witch, and the Wardrobe
- Pigs Eat Farmer

And you can find many more at pointer.org.

And here's an all-too-familiar headline that may have inspired Merle Drown: *Woman Claims Spousal Abuse as Defense in Murder Case*:

SHE KNEW BETTER

NO EFFECTIVE ANTIDOTE IS KNOWN, BUT
SYMPTOMATIC TREATMENT MAY BE EFFECTIVE

In the morning she found Ray at the kitchen table cleaning her fecal matter from the barrel of his .22-250. He didn't look up. Last night he'd rolled his sleeves to his elbows revealing the long tendons, powerful muscles, deep blue veins. Now the cuffs were bottomed tight around his wrists.

"You're up early," she said. She felt as if she'd tumbled in the dryer all night.

"Five hundred dollars for this varmint rifle, I have to keep it clean," he said. Then he looked up, eyes as small and dark as the end of his gun. "I'm disappointed. I expected my coffee by now."

Half-listening to the grinder's whirling whine, she watched him fill the magazine with bullets from his shirt pocket. *Never clean a loaded gun.* A Ray Rule. She didn't have to tell him. She knew better than to tell him anything he already knew. Another Ray Rule.

Bringing his cup, she walked carefully to avoid showing her pain. "That's my good girl," he said. He took the cup, drank most of it down hot, and pinched her butt.

She flinched. Ray smiled at her and licked his full lips, reminding her how hungrily he'd kissed her that first night, all over. All over.

"Today's our anniversary," she said. "It's—"

"You know better. Five years."

When they'd moved to the old sheep ranch, Ray had bought the rifle to keep the coyotes from killing sheep. But they raised no sheep. Ray hated animals.

"Ray," she said as she poured coffee in his insulated cup for his drive to work, "I'm going to finish cleaning in the barn today. Is there anything you want to keep?"

"Ray Rule: you know better than to bother me with women's work."

A bookkeeper, she finished the pharmacy accounts by noon, put on dishwashing gloves, and went to the barn.

She slit the plastic pack on a Livestock Protection Collar, like slicing chicken breast from the bone. Yesterday, she'd found the dusty box of the collars labeled, *For use on sheep to kill depredating coyotes.*

She took the collar into the kitchen. So as not to ruin her good kitchen knife, she pricked the black rubber pouch with a needle and squeezed the Compound 1080 into a cup. It was, as she had read online, the color of strong coffee and amounted to a tablespoon, enough for six men, sufficient for Ray.

When he came in the house at five-thirty, gripping a bottle of Bordeaux by the neck, she poured him his hot coffee. She knew he wouldn't kiss her, so she waited until he'd drunk half the cup before she led him to the barn.

"Why didn't you chuck that old box of poison sheep collars?" Ray said.

She put the two white straps of a Protection Collar over her head and secured the Velcro. The black rubber pouch sat at her neck like a broach. "These collars wouldn't protect the sheep who wore them because the depredating coyote would bite through the pouch to the sheep's throat," she said.

"What the hell are you up to?"

"I want you to know I'm pregnant."

He leaned against a pole, vomited, and slid to the floor.

"Ray Rule," he said. "You'll pay—"

"It's undetectable," she said.

He vomited, fouled his pants, and twisted like a broken-backed snake. She took his coffee cup into the house to rinse it. She opened the wine. She'd let it breathe, then drink a glass, just one, with the baby coming and all.

What a disturbing opening line, delivered without flinching. We understand the terror our wife is living with; we understand her determination to take care of herself, and, more importantly, her unborn child. We hear her tell this monster, "You will not abuse my child. End of story!"

Flash and Blood

Urban legends are oral stories based on hearsay and passed along as truth. Some of the current circulating urban legends that you may or may not know about include Elvis in the Witness Protection Program; a former first lady stealing White House furniture; alligators in the sewer system of a city near you; baby in the microwave; hippo eats dwarf; and killer in the backseat. A good story is always worth retelling. The Wily Home Invader—the story of a killer already in the house—is another. Write a short-short horror story based on an urban legend in the manner of, say, Edgar Allan Poe, Stephen King, or Shirley Jackson. You won't have much time to let the horror and tension build. Use some familiar horror tropes in fresh, unusual ways. The chain saw, the ghost in the mirror, abandoned houses, mad scientists, cemeteries, scratching at the wall, and so on. Make us afraid, very afraid. Here's a quote from the master Alfred Hitchcock: "There is no terror in the bang, only in the anticipation of it."

Here's Corey Ginsberg's unsettling story which plays on the familiar puritanical conceit that girls having fun must be punished.

HOME

The man with the knife snuck in through the unlocked back door while the girls were unloading groceries in the kitchen. As he'd done at the other four rental properties that day, he found the bedroom nearest the exit. His childhood trips to this beach town had taught him there was usually one suite apart from the others, a twin bedroom with a shit view, the latecomer's penalty.

Although his instinct told him the room would be empty, the man had developed a habit of peering around bends. Innocuous pink décor, framed stock photo of a sailboat, suitcases left open-faced, spewing clothes onto an oatmeal carpet. In one smooth, practiced motion, he slid in and wedged himself beneath the bed nearest the door.

The house reeked of bleach's corrosive efforts to cover up what had come before. The other rentals had had the same synonymous stink of being used for six and a half days, then forsaken, scoured, and turned over to another family. His blood-soaked shirt was an affront to the cleanliness.

The girls were down the hall, their footsteps a pitter-pattering of sheep hooves. From this angle the man with the knife could see the base of the dresser, heels of high-lacing boots, and mounds of discarded clothing that undoubtedly cost more than its worth in wear. He studied a cashmere sweater that had collapsed next to the night-stand, then ran the fingers of his free hand over the corner of the untucked sheet. He swallowed, throat constricting with desire, and willed himself to contain his rapture.

It was off-season. February, dead time. The girls must have gotten a deal on the rental. Their screams would be washed over by the clean suck of the Atlantic just yards away. Beachfront properties were good that way. The other four had been forgiving of the momentary outburst. A slight bleep on an otherwise clean cardiogram.

The certainty of what was to unfold calmed the man. He reveled in the perfection of his pattern. Each cookie-cutter house a separate stage for a stabbing soliloquy, a contained masterpiece that would be remembered long after the cops and cleaning crews left.

The girls giggled as they joked about someone named Josh. Their bleating, their banter. The man adjusted the folded corner of the duvet. His mother had had similar bedding. A woman of many sensibilities but little common sense. A woman with perfectly folded linens kept in a locked box that traveled with them, from vacation house to vacation house, with each of her five boyfriends. He recalled the interchangeable father figures, each worse than his predecessor. The man had never been allowed to touch her precious bedding, let alone to lie on it.

"I'm going to shower," one of the girls shouted.

The man let his fingers absorb the softness of the sheets. He traced the knife blade along the stubborn fold that refused to hang straight. The knife's terrible beauty, its utter finality. He was closer than ever to finding home.

———

A cool and restrained narrator gives us a glimpse into the deranged mind of a monster. While the worst thing that can happen doesn't happen on the page, it does happen in our imaginations.

—

And here are some more exercises to keep you blissfully writing:

Hot Flash

"The heart has its reasons which reason knows nothing of." With Pascal's quote in mind, write a very short romance story. Good girl/bad boy? Or vice versa. Married man and mistress? Post-apocalyptic romance? Transgender romance. (Please, no zombie rom-coms! Oh, why the hell not!) Romance stories are often fantasies for the reader and involve slightly larger and more stunning characters than we are used to in realistic fiction. But they don't have to be.

Flashback

Begin your story with one of the following lines that we might expect to find at the end of a story:

- And then I woke up and it was only a dream.
- And they all lived happily ever after.
- And then the guillotine sliced my neck.
- And that's how I came to be here with you.
- He could struggle no longer and slept.

Flash Drive

Your short-short story takes place in a car or a pickup or an RV. On the road—the great American myth, the romance of the highway. Your central character is driving. He's alone or with a companion or with several. What does he see out the window? In the rearview mirror? The radio is on. What's he listening to? Where is he going? Why there? What is the promise at the end of the road? What's the weather like? What time of day is it? Is there trouble up ahead? Tension in the car? How much gas is left in the tank?

Flash Forward

Alice Munro said, "I can't see that people develop and arrive somewhere. I just see people living in flashes." With that notion in mind, begin your story with a person in crisis, struggling to achieve some breakthrough or some relief, and then, just like that, launch your character into the future. The reader will fill in the interim. Then she was blind; now she can see.

Flash-O-Matic

Simply take one item at random from each column in the chart that follows. Column A lists characters by their occupation. Column B tells us what the character wants. Column C presents us with a scene that will constitute some or all of your very short story. Ask the questions provoked by your selections. What high school does she work at? What was the insult? Why does the car need cleaning? Give the character a name and an address. Ask yourself, or ask your character, what are the obstacles in the way.

A	B	C
1. High school guidance counselor	1. Wants to be happy for once	1. Writes a suicide note for a neighbor
2. Video game tester	2. Wants to end his/her marriage	2. Can't stop crying
3. Volcanologist	3. Wants to nail this job interview	3. Silently repeats a prayer
4. Sous chef	4. Wants to find the killer	4. Pretends to be someone he or she is not
5. Veterinarian	5. Wants to earn his/her mother's/father's respect	5. Flips a coin
6. Chiropractor	6. Wants to avenge an insult	6. Visits a fortune-teller
7. Mail carrier	7. Wants to win the heart of X	7. Spies on the house next door
8. Flight attendant	8. Wants to continue living a lie	8. Sleeps with a crucifix
9. TV meteorologist	9. Wants to save his/her self-destructive child	9. Makes up the dreams he or she writes in a journal
10. Psychologist	10. Wants to be honest with the one person who matters	10. Washes the car at three in the morning

11. Personal trainer	11. Wants to die with dignity, not like this	11. Sits alone in the dark, singing jazz standards
12. Massage therapist	12. Wants a life like the one he/she tells people he/she has	12. Pretends to be deaf

Flashlight

"Life is a comedy for those who think and a tragedy for those who feel." That's a quote I've seen variously ascribed to Jean de la Bruyère, Molière, Horace Walpole, Jean Racine, Anonymous, and F. Scott Fitzgerald. And I'd always thought it was Groucho Marx who said it. Life is a mystery for *both* thinkers and feelers. In this very short comic mystery story you will illuminate a mystery with a light touch. You'll need to make up your sleuth and the conundrum she's attempting to solve. She works alone or has a partner.

Flash Gordon

I like my sci-fi over easy. My intro to the genre came from TV—the *Flash Gordon* serials starring Buster Crabbe. Here was a world of intergalactic space travel where combatants still used swords and dressed in medieval armor. Not so very different than *Star Wars*, I suppose. Sci-fi is realistic and unlike fantasy. It has to be plausible. It extrapolates from scientific trends, and real science must be a part of science fiction. If you were hypothesizing based on current trends in actual science, your short-short story might include a future where anyone could start his own pandemic, where privacy is nonexistent (we're almost there), where antibiotics are ineffective, where all our satellites have been vaporized by solar flares, where climate change has resulted in the inundation of coastal cities and the eradication of island chains, and where robots find it easy to manipulate us and kill us. So write your sci-fi flash in a world not so far, far away. Make it 451 words in honor of Ray Bradbury.

The Word Becomes Flash

Here are some quotes. Choose one or more that sound intriguing, and don't think too much at first. Just start writing. I'm guessing that themes will present themselves to you and that you'll discover some intriguing characters.

- "There is a crack in everything; that's how the light gets in." Leonard Cohen

- "I don't know why we are here, but I'm pretty sure it is not in order to enjoy ourselves." Ludwig Wittgenstein

- "Sorrow is so easy to express and yet so hard to tell." Joni Mitchell

- "Memory is the way we keep telling ourselves our stories—and telling other people a somewhat different version of our stories." Alice Munro

- "They fuck you up, your mum and dad. They may not mean to, but they do." Philip Larkin

The (Fl)Ashtray

In a letter of literary advice, Chekhov once offered the following suggestion: *You could write a story about this ashtray, for example, and a man and a woman. But the man and the woman are always the two poles of your story. The North Pole and the South. Every story has these two poles—he and she.* To see what can be done when you take this seed from Chekhov and plant it in your imagination, read Raymond Carver's poem "The Ashtray" in his collection *Where Water Comes Together with Other Water*. Put your two characters together at the table with the ashtray. Let the trouble surface and write the scene. Let them talk. Write it twice. Once from his POV. Once from hers.

The Outro

S o you've been writing like crazy, and you've discovered the joy of making up people and places that didn't exist before. You've learned that the first act of writing is paying attention, making yourself susceptible to the provocative world. Any object—this teacup full of thumbtacks, let's say—or any person—that orangey fellow with the peculiar hairweave over by the eggplants—can provoke a story. You know that you can sit in any public place, glance around, let your gaze settle on an intriguing person, and begin to build a complex flesh-and-blood character from this person you know nothing about, except what you can surmise from her appearance and behavior.

Maybe you start by giving her a name and an address, by following her home—in your notebook, of course—we're snooping, not stalking. You wander from room to room and note the details of the place, every one of which reveals her character. You ask questions: Does she live alone? Have pets? Is she taking care of herself? You look for the clues that will lead to some answers. You write down anything at all that helps you get to know her. And from your gathered evidence, you imagine the trouble she is having in her private life, the trouble she lets no one else know about.

You're having fun with words and with the music of language, and you've learned that the intimidating blank page is easier to face when you have a self-imposed template of, say, five hundred words and in a familiar form, perhaps, but one you've never tried before. Those nonliterary forms—texts meant to convey messages, facts, or information—are all around you, like the notes on supermarket bulletin boards, book jacket blurbs, movie reviews, wedding vows, greeting cards, astrology columns, job applications, résumés, police blotters, billboards, literary criticism, catalogues, business cards, assembly instructions, and so it goes.

And you have learned, or will soon, that you don't have a problem coming up with characters, settings, themes, and plots for stories, but you do have the problem of not being able to write efficiently enough to tell them all. You're writing against the clock. So when you finish the story about Elias Cobb, the man who's treating his rosacea with Dr. Campbell's Arsenic Complexion Wafers, and his agitated e-mail correspondence with Becky Ofori of Ghana whose father was murdered by a polygamous tribal leader, whose mother died of grief, who desperately needs cash to rescue her siblings, and is willing to sell her father's stockpile of gold ingots for pennies on the dollar, if only Elias could send her a small cash advance, when you finish the story, you know what to do. Begin the next one. The more you write, the more you will want to write. And all the writing you do today, goes to all the writing you will ever do. You know that, so you sit yourself in the chair, you face the blank page, you put down a word, any word. You watch your character closely. Her name's Kimberly, you decide. She's standing at the hostess's station at that new French bistro on the boulevard. Her child is in a stroller. His name is Jaden. No, Theo. That's better. The hostess puts down the phone and makes a note on the reservation chart. She looks at Kimberly, who looks to be at her wit's end. What's going on? you wonder. You watch. You wait. Kimberly says, "Do you have a children's menu and a full bar?"

Acknowledgments

I WANT to thank the authors who generously participated in the writing of this book. And thanks to my agent Bill Clegg, and to my editor, Jill Bialosky, who once again made this a far better book than it would have been. Thanks to my friend Dick McDonough, without whom I would have had no writing career. And thanks to Kim Bradley, friend and storyteller; Dave Cole, sculptor, morel forager, friend, and copy editor; and Drew Elizabeth Weitman, editorial assistant extraordinaire. And thank you, Teddy and Jim Bob Jones, Cully and Susan Perlman, Jill Coupe, Peter Stravlo and Peggy McGivern, Karen and Garry Kravit, David and Rosie Norman, Kimberly and Jeremy Rowan, Bruce Harvey and Liz Kortlander. And thanks to the kids who bring so much joy into our lives: Theo and Phoebe and Meena and Nyla and James and Caleb and Charlie.

About the Authors

STEVE ALMOND spent seven years as a newspaper reporter in Texas and Florida before writing his first book, the story collection *My Life in Heavy Metal* (Grove Press, 2002). His nonfiction book *Candyfreak* (Algonquin Books, 2004) was a *New York Times* bestseller. His short fiction has been included in the *Best American Short Stories* and *Pushcart Prize* anthologies, and his collection *God Bless America* (Lookout Books, 2011) won the Paterson Fiction Prize. He writes regularly for the *New York Times Magazine* and the *Boston Globe*.

LYNNE BARRETT's third story collection is *Magpies* (Carnegie Mellon, 2011). She edits the *Florida Book Review*, and her recent work appears in *Necessary Fiction*, *Rose Red Review*, the *Southern Women's Review*, *Fort Lauderdale* magazine, *Fifteen Views of Miami,* and *Trouble in the Heartland: Stories Inspired by the Songs of Bruce Springsteen*.

STEVEN BARTHELME has published two books of short stories, the most recent of which is *Hush Hush* (Melville House, 2012), a memoir *Double Down,* coauthored with his brother Frederick (Houghton Mifflin, 1999) and an essay collection, *The Early Posthumous Work* (Red Hen Press, 2010).

Don Bullens photographs rock concerts, the red tiled roofs of Italy, details of Gaudi architecture, and a macro photographic series of jellyfish and other aquatic oddities from aquariums in the U.S. and Europe. He is attracted to down-and-out diners and ghost advertising but also to tropical birds, and the bees, butterflies, and flowers of the Northeast, where he lives and teaches photography at Worcester State University.

Robert Busby's stories have appeared in *Arkansas Review, Cold Mountain Review, Mississippi Noir* (Akashic, 2016), *PANK, Sou'wester,* and *Surreal South '11.* He has worked as a band saw operator, a produce clerk, a bookseller, a driving school instructor, and a satellite television technician.

Cynthia Chinelly teaches writing at Florida International University.

Tom Demarchi teaches in the Department of Language and Literature at Florida Gulf Coast University. His work has appeared in the *Writer's Chronicle,* the *Miami Herald, Quick Fiction,* the *Pinch, Gulfstreaming,* the *Southeast Review, GulfShore Life,* and other publications. When not teaching or writing, Tom's busy directing the Sanibel Island Writers Conference.

Merle Drown has written three novels, *Plowing Up a Snake* (Doubleday, 1982), *The Suburbs of Heaven* (Soho Press, 2000), and *Lighting the World* (Triquarterly, 2001). He edited *Meteor in the Madhouse,* the posthumous novellas of Leon Forrest. Over thirty pieces from his collection-in-progress *Shrunken Heads,* miniature portraits of the famous among us, have appeared in *Kenyon Review, Night Train, Bound Off,* and other publications. He has received fellowships from the National Endowment for the Arts and the New Hampsire State Council on the Arts.

DENISE DUHAMEL's most recent book of poetry is *Scald* (Pittsburgh, 2017). *Blowout* (Pittsburgh, 2013) was a finalist for the National Book Critics Circle Award. Duhamel, a recipient of fellowships from the Guggenheim Foundation and the National Endowment for the Arts, is a professor at Florida International University in Miami.

MICHÈLE-JESSICA (M.J.) FIÈVRE was born in Port-au-Prince and is the founding editor of *Sliver of Stone* magazine, and the author of *A Sky the Color of Chaos* (Beating Windward, 2015). She obtained her MFA from the creative writing program at Florida International University.

COREY GINSBERG's work has appeared in such publications as *PANK*, the *Cream City Review, Subtropics*, and *Third Coast*, among others. Her nonfiction was listed as a Notable in the *Best American Essays* in 2012 and 2014.

JASON MARC HARRIS teaches creative writing, folklore, and literature for the English Department at Texas A&M University. His stories have appeared in *Arroyo Literary Review, Cheap Pop, Every Day Fiction, Masque & Spectacle, Midwestern Gothic*, and *Psychopomp* magazine.

NATHAN LESLIE's ten books include *Root and Shoot* (Texture Press, 2016), *Sibs* (Aqueous Press, 2014), and *The Tall Tale of Tommy Twice* (Atticus Books, 2012). His work has appeared in hundreds of literary magazines. He edited *The Best of the Web, Pedestal* magazine, and interviews for *Prick of the Spindle*. His story appeared in *Best Small Fictions 2016*.

BONNIE LOSAK-JIMENEZ is an attorney in Miami, Florida, and an MFA candidate at Florida International University. Her creative nonfiction piece "A Lack of Buoyancy" was published in *Hippo-campus* magazine. She has also published book reviews in *Gulf Stream* magazine and the *Florida Book Review*. She lives and writes in Miami Beach.

RACHEL LURIA is a Pushcart Prize nominee and two-time winner of the South Carolina Fiction Project. She is an associate professor at Florida Atlantic University's Wilkes Honors College. Her work has appeared in the *Normal School*, *Harpur Palate*, *Sport Literate*, *Saw Palm*, *Phoebe*, *Dash Literary Journal*, *Yemassee*, and others. To read samples of her work, visit rachelluria.wordpress.com

LEE MARTIN has published three memoirs, most recently *Such a Life* (University of Nebraska Press, 2012). He is also the author of four novels, including *Late One Night* (Dzanc Books, 2016), *Break the Skin* (Crown, 2011), and *The Bright Forever* (Broadway Books, 2005), a finalist for the 2006 Pulitzer Prize in Fiction. He teaches in the MFA program at Ohio State University.

CAMPBELL MCGRATH is the author of nine books of poetry, including *Spring Comes to Chicago* (Ecco, 1996), *Florida Poems* (Ecco, 2001), and most recently *Poems for the Twentieth Century* (Ecco, 2016) He has received many of America's major literary prizes for his work, including the Kingsley Tufts Award, a Guggenheim Fellowship, a MacArthur Fellowship, a USA Knight Fellowship, and a Witter Bynner Fellowship from the Library of Congress.

BRENDA MILLER is the author of five essay collections, most recently *An Earlier Life* (Ovenbird Books, 2016). She also coauthored with Suzanne Paola *Tell It Slant: Creating, Refining, and Publishing Creative Nonfiction* (McGraw-Hill, 2003) and *The Pen and The Bell: Mindful Writing in a Busy World* (Skinner House

Books, 2012). Her work has received six Pushcart Prizes. She is a professor of English at Western Washington University, and a member of the associate faculty at the Rainier Writing Workshop.

DEBRA MONROE is the author of six books, which have won many awards, including the Flannery O'Connor Award. Her work has appeared in many periodicals, including *Glimmer Train*, the *Georgia Review*, the *New York Times*, Longreads.com, the *American Scholar*, and *Guernica*.

LEONARD NASH received a Florida Book Award for *You Can't Get There from Here and Other Stories* (Kitsune Books, 2007). His work has appeared in the *South Dakota Review*, the *Seattle Review*, *Fort Lauderdale Magazine*, *15 Views of Miami* (Burrow Press, 2014), *Gulf Stream*, and elsewhere.

DAVID NORMAN lives in Madison, Wisconsin. His stories have appeared in *Image, Southern Humanities Review, American Literary Review*, and elsewhere. He received a Pushcart Prize nomination from *Gulf Stream* and an honorable mention from *Glimmer Train*. His writing and music are available on his website: www.davidrnorman.com.

DAVID REICH is the author of the novel *The Antiracism Trainings* (BlazeVOX, 2010). His prose has been appearing in literary magazines since the 1970s—*North American Review, Transatlantic Review, Brilliant Corners, Gargoyle, Beyond Baroque*, the *Smith*, and others. He is working on a memoir of his service as executor of a former girlfriend's will.

JAROD ROSELLÓ is a Cuban-American cartoonist, writer, and teacher. He is the author and artist of the graphic novel *The Well-Dressed Bear Will (Never) Be Found* (Publishing Genius Press,

2015), and the illustrated novel *How We Endure* (Jellyfish Highway Press, 2018). He teaches comics and fiction in the creative writing program at the University of South Florida and runs the Latinx publisher Bien Vestido Press.

NATALIA RACHEL SINGER's story "Honeycomb" was the winning entry in the World's Short Short Story Contest of 1992, sponsored by Florida State University's graduate program in creative writing. The author of *Scraping By in the Big Eighties* (University of Nebraska Press, 2004), a memoir, and several stories and essays, Singer is a professor of English and creative writing at St. Lawrence University.

JASON SKIPPER is the author of the novel *Hustle* (Press 53, 2011), which was selected as a finalist for the PEN Center USA Award for Fiction. His stories have appeared in numerous publications, and he has received awards and recognition from *Zoetrope: All Story, Glimmer Train,* and *Crab Orchard Review.* He studied in the Master's program at Miami of Ohio and in the Ph.D. in Creative Writing Program at Western Michigan University. He lives in Tacoma, Washington, where he teaches creative writing at Pacific Lutheran University

MARY SLEBODNIK has an MFA from Florida International University and teaches high school English.

RENNIE SPARKS is one half of the Handsome Family, creepy country cave singers.

DANIEL STAESSER graduated from Florida State University in 2001 with a degree in creative writing. He currently resides in southwest Florida with his wife and son. He has spent the last ten years teaching English/language arts. This is his second published short story.

Leslie Taylor teaches high school English in Broward County, Florida. He also sponsors his school's literary journal.

Julie Marie Wade is the author of eight collections of poetry and prose, most recently *SIX: Poems* (Red Hen Press, 2016), selected by C. D. Wright as the winner of the AROHO/To the Lighthouse Poetry Prize, and *Catechism: A Love Story* (Noctuary Press, 2016). She teaches in the creative writing program at Florida International University in Miami and reviews regularly for the *Rumpus* and *Lambda Literary Review*.

Ruthann Ward practices psychotherapy in Miami, Florida, and is a member of the fridaynightwriters at Florida International University. This is Ruthann's first publication.

Tom Williams is the author of three books of fiction: *The Mimic's Own Voice* (Main Street Rag, 2012), *Don't Start Me Talkin'* (Curbside Splendor Publishing, 2014), and *Among the Wild Mulattos and Other Tales* (Texas Review Press, 2015). He lives in Kentucky with his wife and children.

Story Credits and Permissions

Natalia Rachel Singer's "Honeycomb" first appeared in *Micro Fiction*, edited by Jerome Stern. Copyright by the author and reprinted with the permission of the author.

Jason Skipper's "Ghosts" first appeared in *Phoebe*. Copyright by the author and reprinted with the permission of the author.

Mary Slebodnik's "Hometown Market's Delicious Fried Chicken Serves: Anyone Willing to Pay $23.00 a box ($11.99 after 7:00 P.M.)" appears here for the first time. Copyright by the author and reprinted with the permission of the author.

Rennie Sparks's "Cathedrals" first appeared on the Handsome Family album *Through the Trees*. Copyright by the author and printed with the permission of the author. "Lake Geneva" appeared on the Handsome Family album *Milk and Scissors*. Copyright by the author and printed with the permission of the author.

Daniel Staesser's "Narcissus Redeemed" appears here for the first time. Copyright by the author and printed with the permission of the author.

Leslie Taylor's "Supper Club Blackmail" appears here for the first time. Copyright by the author and reprinted with the permission of the author.

Julie Marie Wade's "Y" first appeared as a winner of the 2004 Chicago Literary Award for Poetry in *Another Chicago Magazine*. Copyright by the author and reprinted with the permission of the author. Her "Portrait of the Child after the Fall" first appeared in *Cadillac Cicatrix*. Copyright by the author and printed with the permission of the author.